MAPPING LOVE

Ashwiny Iyer Tiwari is an artist, filmmaker and writer. A gold medallist in Commercial Arts from Sophia Polytechnic, Mumbai, she spent over a decade in the advertising world, telling stories for the biggest brands in India and Southeast Asia. She has won several advertising 'craft' awards across the world for her layered ideas and in-depth understanding of human psychology at the grassroot level. She directed the critically acclaimed, award-winning short film, 'What's for Breakfast?', 'Brothers' and 'Ghar ki Murgi' (Taken for Granted). Her first highly acclaimed Hindi feature film, 'Nil Battey Sannata' also known as, 'The New Classmate' helped her spread the message of 'education for all' and won Indian and International gender sensitivity awards. She remade it in Tamil as, 'Amma Kanakku' (Mother's Calculation). Her next movie, 'Bareilly Ki Barfi,' a slice of life romantic comedy continued her passion for storytelling and won many popular and critics' awards. With her latest widely acclaimed movie, 'Panga', she started an important conversation on sports and motherhood. Making her own path with her simple yet mindful outlook towards life, she is a conscious knowledge researcher, traveller and seeker for life. This is her first book.

MAPPING LOVE

ASHWINY IYER TIWARI

Published by
Rupa Publications India Pvt. Ltd 2021
7/16, Ansari Road, Daryaganj
New Delhi 110002

Sales centres:
Allahabad Bengaluru Chennai
Hyderabad Jaipur Kathmandu
Kolkata Mumbai

Copyright © Ashwiny Iyer Tiwari 2021

All rights reserved.

No part of this publication may be reproduced, transmitted,
or stored in a retrieval system, in any form or by any means,
electronic, mechanical, photocopying, recording or otherwise,
without the prior permission of the publisher.

This is a work of fiction. Names, characters, places and incidents are either the
product of the author's imagination or are used fictitiously and any resemblance
to any actual person, living or dead, events or locales is entirely coincidental.

ISBN: 978-93-5333-791-9

First impression 2021

10 9 8 7 6 5 4 3 2 1

The moral right of the author has been asserted.

Printed at Thomson Press India Ltd., Faridabad

This book is sold subject to the condition that it shall not, by way
of trade or otherwise, be lent, resold, hired out, or otherwise circulated,
without the publisher's prior consent, in any form of binding or
cover other than that in which it is published.

*It tastes like a beginning.
I said, 'I can hear hope'.*

PART 1

5:45 PM, Lucknow

As I get off the station, a sudden chill in my spine reminds me of all the things I have missed. Often life takes you to a junction where you are not sure about the turn. The turn seems to be a choice you need to make. This time I am bound. Both my heart and mind seem to tiptoe around uncertainty. There is a lot in my undiscovered mind that needs to open. May be this is the reason a few things happen in life to bring you back to your senses. To get a hold of you and make you aware that life is not about the choices you make but the choices that make you. Here I am, living my life looking at the rear-view mirror, driving to the end of the beginning of where I started.

My body still hurts.

REMEMBER

We often pass the same lanes. The same houses. The same trees which have withered or are blooming with happiness. The birds find the same trees to build their nests tirelessly. When I was 14 years old, I used to take a similar road to my house a couple of times, every day. Walking on this road was a time I would cherish. I loved being on my own. It was a wonderful feeling for a rebel like me who loved her freedom and just wanted to run away from the constant nagging love of her 'Devi' Amma and the only other member of the family—a 'straight-faced' father, who hardly mattered in my scheme of things.

I was waiting. Waiting eagerly to graduate and move out of this place to the US of A and be a master of my own destiny. Many like me who could afford a scholarship wanted to go and I was no different. The best part of being in the West is that you know, unless there is some unforeseen agenda, you are not really going to come back. Imagine, spending so much of money, working part-time, double time to pay off your stay and then coming back? Not a good idea at all. Deep in my heart, I knew that I would find someone there and spend the rest of my life as a green card citizen.

Today, none of the above matters as I walk on a lane I had heard of in conversations but never had a chance to see. The trees must have got older. Flowers never age, so there are new ones blooming with happiness. They seem to be welcoming me. Everything is the same. But there is something missing today even in this unknown lane, a voice calling out my name. That voice which never got lost even during the rains. Today, I can wholeheartedly admit that I enjoyed the sound of wind mixed with my Amma's constant argument on topics that we enjoyed discussing. I constantly complained about life. We spoke to each other like friends who could not share every secret but still knew a lot about each other. And then one day, she was gone, without saying a word, and my world came crashing down. When I was flying in the sky, she pulled me back like a force of nature. It was her way of telling me to go deep inside the layers of the earth and find my roots.

On the upper part of the tree, however, there were leaves that were disjointed. While my mother was nurturing me, my relationship with my father was strung together with not more than two words. He was the Head of Department

(Archaeology), mostly busy travelling to places to search for something or the other. Except tending to my tuition fee, he never had the time to know me. Amma was the only bridge of comfort. The distance with him only increased when I moved. Later, I would often wonder how a person so full of life can be taken away in a car accident, while nothing happens to the person driving. He was the one who chose to take her for some important work in Delhi; he did not need her there. She might as well have stayed at home waiting for him like all the other times and she would have continued being with me, travelling and tending to her green babies. The one thing she loved.

This is my state of mind.

Hard to forget. Harder still to remember.

1

There is so much chaos, but the palatial station seems to be resting in peace in all its old-world architectural charm. After travelling for almost 36 hours, the tired-looking face with a pixie cut, the foreign-returned-confused-Desi with a big red American bag is trying to find her way out of this mayhem of people walking past with their definite itineraries.

I have been struggling with a lot of problems. And right now, my biggest problem boils down to only one word—life. My parents named me 'Oorja'—an energy that can take a variety of forms.

I wonder what my parents must have discussed when they decided on this name. I am indeed a form of bubbling energy but for all the wrong reasons. None of which my Amma would even think of, even in her wildest dreams.

Wasting my energy on the wrong men.

I fall in love very easily, with any man who gives me a little importance. And when this saga of men after men and hardly any work bores me, my energy does take a wide variety of forms. Fighting for the wrong causes. Swinging words. Spending a fortune online shopping. Binging on mouth-watering food. Indulging with different men who come my way, when in fact, I believe in monogamy; I am in and out of love every few months until I get bored of it. So, for the past six years, I have been leading a lonely life with multiple wrong men. I don't consider myself a nymphomaniac, but my relationships still qualify me as a loner who has also been struggling with many issues with herself. I have this intense fear of being judged or evaluated by others and I constantly wonder what others are thinking about me. I hate criticism and rejection, and that's why before someone rejects me, I reject them.

Wasting my energy on the work I am not in love with is yet another issue I am dealing with. Having done my video course and having majored in travel writing, I was working for a world-class travel channel, something that elicits a 'wow' every time someone hears of it. But no one really knows what is happening inside it, including the dozens of us who was working inside. Everything looked very nice till the milk spilled and I could not clean up my scattered life and I needed a break from it all. I wanted to find my so-called lost self—the same kind we read a lot about. More than ever, there was a lot of unanswered questions that I had to ask my father. My American lifestyle had to change, merging with the air of new India.

I jolt back to the present. It's time for a smoke as I notice many misspelled 'no smoking' boards in our train, which makes me eager for one right now. Unlike ten years ago, now all types of desi-videshi[1] cigarettes are available along with the old beedi and 'paan'[2], a deadly habit my Amma got from her father who was a forest officer. My Amma thought this was his job, for all she could see was him visiting his friends in this jungle while carrying this non-tobacco fascination. One day, while he was out, at the age of 19, finally she tasted this beauty, which was left by mistake in a little tin box on the table, only to be quite fond of it. It's a 'family' thing, she would say, chewing a bite filled with rose and jaggery syrup, with cardamom and peppermint and savouring the flavour right after her meal. The only thing she openly did before my father, since he also loved his after-meal betel leaf with sweet rose paste.

It's all in the family. So, I don't have to be scared even if my father sees me in this avatar. Not that I bother now, after all these years.

I hear a voice while savouring my mild. It's a young man, clad in a white shirt and blue jeans, who wants to

---

[1] Indian and foreign
[2] A mouth freshener

know whether I would need his help to carry my only suitcase and get me a rickshaw. I stare at him as the smoke covers his tired face. In America, you must do everything on your own. I shake my head to signify no, seeing the short stairs I would need to climb to get to the other side and then would love to haggle with a rickshaw driver who has a 'to go, not to go' confused mind. A train has just arrived and there is a wave of people standing to pounce. For every single person, there would be a minimum of two to drop or receive them from the station. It was so in our family too.

Mrs Sudha Chaturvedi always went to drop Mr Vishal Chaturvedi, my hypochondriac, regimented father, to the station on a light blue vintage scooter. I used to sit in the front feeling strong, as if I were riding an army bike, in charge of the three of us. My father's non-stop instructions would blend with the constant honks, so much so that all I could hear in my mind was the 70's rock & roll songs that my Amma enjoyed listening to when father was not around.

Parking the scooter at the fixed place right beside the entrance, Amma and I would follow Father, who would walk as fast as a Panther and it would invariably be difficult to follow him. Amma would run and I would run behind her to finally find him entering a compartment that we would know was his train. Amma would never go inside the compartment. Smiling, through the railing of the second-class compartment window without any touch or a spoken word, she would give him the one-teaspoon oil *mein tala poori* with zero *mirchi aalu sabji*[3].

We would stand like many others on the long platform for the train to leave, patiently hearing his non-stop loud lecture. I would give him this fake teary-eyed 'I miss you' look that would give dear Mrs Chaturvedi a hard time controlling her laughter and then after the train was nowhere in sight, she would scold her daughter Oorja Chaturvedi in English for this abnormal behaviour.

I must confess, I did not hate my father. I just couldn't stand his restricted outlook towards life. He was an archaeologist, how could he be so stuck? Moreover, I always felt he did not love my Amma as much she loved him. Otherwise, why would she need to have this 'what will your father say' attitude?

Breathe in. Breathe out.

She was allowed to ride a scooter because he was forever angry on the road, a rash driver in a small town with a swarm of people on the road. Once he had such a big argument with the owner of a Maruti car that he needed medicines to calm himself down and of course, he missed his train only to go in the non-reserved compartment the next day.

As I climb the broken stairs to the other side, there

---

[3]Flatbread fried in one teaspoon of oil with a zero-spice potato dish

are many questions that are staring at me. What am I going to do now? How will I react when I see my father? I have only taken a couple of steps in this country and I am already thinking about booking my return ticket. This is what happens when there is no one waiting for you.

The autumn sun covers you like a blanket and even after wearing these Made-in-America cooling sunglasses, it is getting increasingly difficult to see what's in front of me. I manage to squeeze my eyes to ask a rickshaw fellow, 'Bhaiyya[4], will you go to Vrindawan Colony?' He does not understand what I just said. I repeat, this time not with the American accent I had unknowingly acquired. It sounds funny but I enjoy talking in a Desi avatar after a long time. He nods his head. I do not understand whether it is a yes or a no. I ask him again. He does the same thing. This time I assume without asking too many questions and dump my suitcase, rucksack and myself into the rickshaw. 'How much will you take?' is my first question, staring at him in the mirror stuck with heart-shaped love stickers. Finally, I see a betel leaf-filled squeaky face telling me 'sattar'[5] as he looks at the mirror and adjusts his hair. I am so used to the dollar that these seventy rupees seem reasonable and I do not argue. He starts the rickshaw and there I go zooming through the roads.

---

[4]Brother
[5]Seventy

We pass 'khau' gully. Some new shops are open which are selling noodles and momos but most of the old ones with old hand-painted typographic nameplates are closed since they only open in the evening and the rush hour continues till the wee hours of the morning. In every town we stayed, this is a food heaven my Amma and I used to savour every single day when my father was away on his tour.

Why in his absence? Because this was a 'restricted by father' area. 'Don't eat paani puri, you will get loose motions. Don't have bhajiya! God knows where the oil comes from!' Sabudana wada was a big no as apparently it is made of ingredients only he knows about! So, what do we eat at home? We would have bhindi, lauki, batata[6] and dal chawal everyday of our life. Of the local production of bhindi every year, I am sure my family must have consumed half of it, if not more. My father was a bhindi aficionado as he believed the vegetable had magical brain-enhancing power. And yet my left brain did not function as per my father's expectation nor was I good at Math. He wanted me to have a lot of okra. He imagined that one day an okra will fall on my head and I will be the Indian version of Newton's story.

There is a sudden jolt.

---

[6]Okra, gourd, potato

Holy cow! The autowallah is trying to save this big animal that randomly crosses the road and stops right in between. He screeches and stops his auto in true movie hero style. There is pin-drop silence while she slowly walks her chosen path, he thinks it's an achievement and gives me a wide red toothy smile as he spits the remaining juice of the paan on the tyre of the 'laal batti'[7] ambassador car which is waiting next to us. I smile back at him, now smoking. His facial expression changes as he switches on the latest remix that is making the most astounding sounds on the black speakers with Bollywood star cut-outs stuck on the inside of his auto, everything contributing to making him feel like a hero in his charming dhinchak[8] world.

As we enter the lane of the colony, a flush of white flowers on an enormous tree shimmers in the evening light. We see houses in the lane but hardly know the people living inside them. I see a middle-aged woman, just like my Amma, standing at the gate waiting for someone. I wish it were her. The last time I met her was when I had come to renew my passport for ten days in a government quarter just before they shifted here for good. That was indeed the last time. I feel good that I could not come back for her funeral; that way I still remember her smiling face, hugging me at the station before I took a train to

---

[7]Red light on the car, signifying an official vehicle
[8]Kitschy

Delhi. She always drove me around to various places, from tuitions to eating out; she insisted that she would drop me to Delhi and that it would be nice to go for a long drive. But since my father too accompanied us for a change, he drove us while we prayed for our lives the entire way. Given an option, she would not travel in a train. She felt they were good for people who could make friends easily. She did not like other people staring at her or trying to strike up a conversation in the long ride. My mother's prayers were answered, and my father bought a blue Maruti Esteem and like the blue scooter, she learnt driving on the roads of Lucknow where every driver was just waiting to have a bull fight. But then, she was a very strong bull.

Finding my way, I finally arrive at this vintage black iron gate. The space for the car is empty. The scooter is nowhere in sight. My Amma's favourite jasmine which always emitted a faint cooling fragrance, welcoming everyone in the evening, looked dead. To me, it reflects that my father was not really bothered about any of my mother's tiny legacies after she left us forever. A huge tree on the side of the gate is still as strong as ever, giving me warmth. I pass the gate feeling a little anxious. The voice of cricket and children playing comfort my chaotic state of mind. An old uncle is staring at me as I pick up my suitcase looking a little confused. I stand in front of a brown door with a faded number eighteen painted on it. It is a worn-out cream bungalow, built when I was in

America. A place I got to know through photos but never visited. It was kept for retirement till my father decided to shift here, quitting his job early and becoming a research consultant. Surrounded by bushes and, I assume, a small vegetable garden in the backyard, this house became a home with my Amma's touch.

Not anymore.

I ring the bell, there is complete silence. There are weird thoughts springing in my vague mind as I look through the window on the side of the door to see if there is anyone at all.

Must have gone to the market.

Must have gone to the university.

Must have gone to a far-off relative's house who he considers close.

Whatever I know of this house or my parents' life are my assumptions from my mother's words and a few photographs of the house. I know about their life from the conversation on the phone with people I have never met. There is a difference between seeing and knowing. In all the transfers, there were two people my father made friends with, a travel agent and a stationery shop owner. So, it is a fair guess that they were my father's only friends, one who used to book and cancel tickets for him and the other who ordered all kinds of books for my bibliophile Amma and father. The habit of reading had flowed in from the bloodstream of my parents and I do need to give them the credit for one wonderful habit they instilled in me. I ring the bell one more time.

No answer.

2

The last time I had spoken to him was four months back when my mother was up in heaven. Agreed, it is far too long to distance yourself from an ageing father when the only one he was dependent on is no longer around. He did give his valuable sperm, knowingly or unknowingly, and I arrived in this world. At twenty-seven, I lost my mother and I was not there for her funeral. The tickets were very expensive for me to click the payment button and destiny did not want me to be here. I am sure Amma knew how I am. I really love people I am close to, but they cannot expect me to be around them all the time. I am attached and yet overtly detached.

My relationship with my father was like Shakespearean father-daughter characters where he deliberately fails. It's just that the father is so busy being responsible for his child that somewhere he forgets his daughter's nature and personality and does not have the will to know her enough. I thought of myself a little like Jessica from *Merchant of Venice*. She had run away from home, tired of her father's autocratic behaviour. I ran way on the pretext of studying further because of an overly protective, quiet father who always wanted to see his daughter around, which sounds good to hear but feels like a noose around your neck after a point.

I consider going to visit my far-off relatives but the very thought of it makes me remember the questions that would invariably be hurled at me, most of which would go unanswered. I decide instead to meet an uncle I had vaguely heard about in telephonic conversations. I assume one set of keys can be found with this man who owns the stationery shop that also doubled as a bookshop since that's how it has been for ages. Amma would always be at home, but what if she stepped out and forgot the keys? My father assumed she had a bad memory. What if there was a fire? What if suddenly an earthquake occurred and the little house we owned crumpled like cardboard? These were some of the thoughts my overly thoughtful father had in mind when he deposited one set of keys with Mr Rajan—the stationery cum book shop owner. I am hungry, tired and just want to open the damn door and plonk myself on *my* bed. Even though, come to think of it, I don't even know if that bed was transported here and it still exists.

It is 8 pm and I am trying to find the bookshop. My bags are at the front door, but since there is hardly any light, no one would bother to steal from a dilapidated house, or so I hope. I buy a bottle of water to quench my thirst. Tap water won't suit my just-returned-from-USA stomach. I notice in our country, especially in smaller towns, if there is a medicine shop in one lane, then there will be multiple medical shops one after the other. If it's a utensil lane, then every other shop in that lane will sell utensils. And who said our country is unorganized? Every lane has a name. Light gully[9], sonar gully[10], peetal gully[11], and then the names of forefathers' gullies. In one of the gullies, named after a person who contributed to education, there was a line of stationery shops. Looking at the white board with bright red capital letters, I smile with a sense of achievement. It read Rajan bookshop.

The shop is swarming with college students, a couple of girls in tight slacks and frilled tees, waiting for their turn to buy a second-hand digest. Hearing their conversation in 'Nawabi Hindi', I guess it is exam time. A busy evening for Mr Rajan!

My father was rather open-minded for his generation, he never bothered what people would say if they did not

---

[9]Lane
[10]Gold lane
[11]Brass lane

have another child. Me, being their only child. My father was strict in his views about family, even stricter in his worldly views, and that's one reason why I could never get along with him. I used to, and perhaps still think from the heart whereas he had a coherent answer for everything in life. In between all this, dear Amma never knew which side to be on, mine or his.

While staring at a wedding procession passing by in this narrow lane and seeing men and women dancing to 'chamak chalo' made me want to do a quick jig with them. No one is going to mind me joining this dance. It's been ages since I have heard or even felt like a part of a group. Or letting go and just dancing like Amma. She used to dance like a peacock at weddings and play the dholak, laughing at everyone's moves. I am a bad dancer but it's just that the enthusiasm on those faces for a second made me want to be a part of it. Over the sound of the band, I hear a voice screaming my name, mispronouncing it, on the top of his voice, 'Oorja!' I turned to see an elderly man with a faint smile and I ask, 'Mr Rajan?' But then suddenly another voice comes from behind, trying to handle the scooter with one hand, interpreting his silent disgusted expression, 'You are *the* Oorja!' I stare at him. The man stares at me. There is a defiant look in his eyes. I found this moment just like a true filmy scene between long-lost brothers but filled with some strange anger.

With the scooter making impatient sounds, he swiftly

hands over the keys to me. I thought I am mannerless, but he is even more so. I look at the bunch of keys tied together with a cardboard keychain that looks like my father's visiting card, wilted and frayed at the edges. 'Dr Vishal Chaturvedi, HOD, Department of Ancient History and Archaeology', it said, with the University emblem and a telephone number printed in blue on the top right corner, all squeezed in a 4 by 6 super white 4 mm rectangle. The scooter is screaming at the top of its voice, it is instigating me to say something. As a formality, I ask him, 'How is Aunty, Uncle?' I do not wait for him to mourn over my mother's death. I am not interested in asking about my father. He stares at me again in silence before replying, 'She is fine, up there with God taking care of her.' His eyes well up with tears. There is silence in the discomfort and, not wanting to prolong this conversation, I look down as he drives off, leaving behind the distinct whiff of bad liquor. Not wasting a second, I run back through the line of sleepy, sad-looking band baaja[12] men with trumpets in their mouth and kerosene lanterns on their heads. I had never asked Amma about Mrs Rajan, her best friend. She had once mentioned her son, who was studying in Delhi and proudly told me that she had told Mrs Rajan, 'My daughter is studying in New York.' The little pleasures moms have in celebrating their children, no matter that

---

[12]Music troupe

the gratification is one-sided.

As soon as I get the keys, I give up and run to the backyard to relieve myself. It is dark. It's my house and no one can question me. Funnily enough, here, you can pee anywhere even when there are 'DO NOT URINATE HERE' signs warning you not to.

Standing up and walking towards the main door under the flickering municipal tube light, I stop for a moment before opening the door to a pitch-black room. In most of our old houses, the switchboard is usually on the top left or right. Mostly right since most of us are righties. We drive right-handed and our body language is usually skewed towards the right. I automatically go to the right side and press the first switch that I touch with my index finger.

The room looks like the room of a man staying alone for years. I dare myself to go to the kitchen. Everything is in its place, suggesting that no one has entered the kitchen in a long time. The plates sit neatly in the steel rack waiting to be used. I open the cabinet below the stove to check that the gas has been turned off. There are some shrivelled onions and garlic lying in a basket. I open the fridge to see no light. Which means he has gone somewhere for a long time. I switch on the button and the wheezing sound of the fridge brings a little momentum to a taciturn house. At this moment, I feel like a detective who is piecing together the story of the missing man in my life. I assume he is still alive or, although angry, the otherwise cold Mr Rajan would have hugged me, thumped his head on my shoulders and cried with a loud 'beta'[13] echoing in my ears.

There is a room for me with empty cupboards hoping to be filled, including a pair of slippers kept under the bed just in case I don't have a pair whenever I return. I wear the slippers and begin exploring the house. In all the years we shifted house, my room was always next to where my parents had their discreet fights. The constant conversations lingered in my mother's mind even after he had slept. 'How was your day today?' 'Are you happy?' 'Do you want to go somewhere for a short vacation?' These were some questions that my mother longed for, but these were words that were never uttered from a mouth which only had words to say about himself. One would think that a marriage means to unify. However, seeing them share a compartmentalized life together, thanks to their opposite natures, was unlike my perception of what a marriage is.

When you are selfish and only thinking about your happiness, you don't really want to take care of the relationship you are in or you enter into by default. My first stint of independence began after leaving my parents. I did not want anything to bind me like an old book, where it takes a lot of effort to tear the pages. For most of my years, in one relationship or another, I felt like a

---

[13]Child

goldfish out of a bowl, scared that I would be asked to behave in a certain way, change my way of living. I would end relationships due to these fears, so much so that I never allowed any man to stay for more than a night in my house. I wanted everything my way. I hated when strangers used my bathroom, messed it up, never put things in the kitchen the way they should be. In time, I realized I was the confused, contradictory person who could not stay alone for long. I am still trying to acknowledge my bewilderment about my place in this world. I am still falling head over heels for the difficult men. Incidentally, one of them had made me take a hard decision.

Amma understood me well enough to give me my space. My father did not. He thought my mother had not given me the right education and was the reason for my anti-social behaviour. When I was young, I would get these fanciful ideas. I would just look at the moon and say, 'Why can't I have a ladder so I could just climb and meet the moon every day?' I would love writing for hours closed in my room. But when it was time for my father to come home, my otherwise not-so-disturbing Amma would nag me to open the door. I displayed moody behaviour most of the time. On some days, I would spend hours just looking at the pouring rain and the sky spilling its affection on everything green. I epitomized a free spirit. I still am and she could have been too, if she had not decided to abide by the rules of a married life.

I lie on the bed looking at the dead fan hovering above me like a hawk looking for its prey. Everything looks silent. I look at her picture in an old frame kept on the desk with books, loads of them, imploring me to open them and read. The dirty fan continues staring at me. If Amma were here, she would not have allowed a single day with an old brown fan. This is my attention span. One moment, I am thinking about books and the next, I am thinking about a fan. My eyes slowly close as I lie on the right side of the bed. That's the side I sense she is still sleeping on. The lamp is still flickering like my fickle mind.

3

I had this habit of waking up once or twice in the middle of the night to switch on the television and watching some tele-marketing humans selling toiletries in the wee hours when most people are sleeping and only some, like me, are awake. I was alone, far away from my mother but she was always with me; if I had even the slightest doubt, there would be a beep on her phone. Unlike most mothers, Amma was tech savvy. A phone call to her in the morning, sometimes a video call, if the Internet at home behaved well, made my day. Still wide awake after all the housework, she would give me a virtual hug. It's the absence of this reliable attachment which makes me emotionally lonely. I am around people; I am still alone.

Dreaming about talking to her from my box apartment in the West, I wake up to realize it is not the American bed I have been sleeping in for the past 16 years. I am in our Indian bed, the one we would get made from Arif Bhai, the local mattress maker every few years. I loved watching him beating the cotton and filling the chequered cotton cloth, pinching and pushing to finally see a 4 by 6 gadda[14], a bed. Everyone had their wish. Amma wanted a harder one for her back. Baba wanted the semi-hard one. As I grew older, I loved the softer one where you could just dive in. The gadda used to be an important gift during marriages. Amma brought four with her when she was married, which lasted for ten years. Along with the gadda, came the rajaai[15]. I was so fond of mother's saree and the smell of old worn out ones that I took one of her handmade quilts to the US.

Still sleeping in Shishuasana[16], I reminisce about her, looking at her black and white photograph now in the morning light. Beside the frame are old Hindi music CDs. The hundred-songs-in-one mp3 CD which Amma loved collecting. The ones she used to ask Baba to get from the highway dhaba[17] every time he was on a road trip. The same ones that truck drivers played to stay awake on long nights, thinking about their loved ones. I wonder what she was thinking when she was humming these old songs. Perhaps

---

[14]Mattress

[15]Blanket

[16]Child pose

[17]A roadside eatery

like the truck driver, she too had some hidden feelings that submerged with the song like a sinking ship. Perhaps she was lost in thoughts like the painted lady looking beautiful amid pink and yellow flowers in the background.

This is the kind of music you love hearing that makes you happy and dance with joy. The same music that makes you morose about life. The same music that creates lasting memories. My mother would watch me sing loudly, creating a shrill behind the closed windows, playing along with me. I spent most of my younger years opening doors to some stimulating experiences with my mother in a small town enveloped with rustiness. Now, it's not her voice or the loud music anymore but a mind that is occupied with a series of pages filled with contradicting emotions, conditioning myself to run away from everything human and non-human that displeases me.

I need to use the toilet again and this time it was in front of me. I have my doubts about what this one will look like. I have this quirk of clicking good bathroom pictures. In all my office travels, the bathroom in luxurious hotels excited me the most. I used to look forward to clicking a picture of a spick and span toilet with attached bath. Some people have a habit of taking pictures of a neatly made bed. I have that too. The bed that looks perfect when you enter a hotel room. And the next morning, the bed has another story to tell. Of the couple who made aggressive love for the first time. Or the traveller on duty who sleeps straight, arms on his chest on one side, leaving the other side untouched. Or the young girl on an office tour jumping into a five-star bed. Owning it. Last night when I slept on this bed, covered with small purple flowers, untouched, without a single wrinkle, it looked lonely. As if no one had slept in it for a while, and it was longing quietly for someone to touch it. I am staring at the bed and then staring at the bathroom. Dragging myself, I open the door to enter a space we all call ours.

Not as bad I imagined it would be. The bathroom needs a little overhaul. The pipes have rusted. The tiles are those trendy vintage-looking ones. I finish and use the flush which is empty. The switch is in the backyard for the municipal and the borewell water. I find it and switch it on for the water to fill in the tank that sits on top of the house, in the shape of a football. Sitting on the steps of a pale off-white netted door overlooking a backyard, I am craving for a daily dose of morning chai, and only one mild cigarette. This Indianness does not change.

In the bustle of street voices, I vaguely remember a dream from last night. A scary tandav, a dance of destruction in my head. It kept playing in my head; my mother was an ardent follower of Shakti. Our house used to gleam during the nine nights that celebrated the Goddess. I never understood the meaning of fasting for her. But loved the 'fast' food that was prepared. The sabudana khichdi, aalu and rajgira puris, the laddu[18]. Every time my mother used to prepare something special during the festival, the first savoury plate would be given to me, not to eat but take to Preeti aunty. Our neighbour, whose house was home for me when my father was transferred to the forest of Central India. A house I have lived the longest, before I shifted to the US. When I was angry, I would go to Preeti Aunty's house. Unfortunately, no one would come to say sorry or pick me up for they knew I was not running away anytime soon. They could catch me in the neighbour's house which was only divided by a wall with fuchsia pink Bougainvillea trees.

Loads of delicious khatta, meetha, teekha[19] food would be covered with a steel plate. I would go with one plate, give it to Aunty who would smile and ask me to wait and bring her own plate of goodies back. But this one time I did not wait for Amma, I opened the lid and ate one laddu and then two and then a kachori. By the time I reached home, my face was stuffed with the exchange of love. India is comforting, it is a place where neighbours know each other. Where notes are exchanged along with food. Where gossip is shared and the little nerve-wracking moments. Where the deepest feelings are exchanged in hushed tones across a gate.

---

[18] Sweet and savoury dishes
[19] Sour, sweet and spicy

As I sit thinking of these moments, the urge for a smoke disappears, but the yearning for chai still lingers on. In a matter of minutes, I find myself ringing the bell next to a door which is already open. I see Mrs Srivastav smiling at me with her beautiful lines by the eyes, made more dignified with gold-rimmed glasses. I hardly smile and enter the house and walk to the kitchen without asking for permission or directions. She follows me quietly. Her kitchen is adorned with new tiles and modular drawers. I assume the taste of food will always remain the same in any Indian middle-class home which has a woman managing the kitchen with loads of love. I feel like she knew that I would knock on the door, seeing as in a small town, when a closed house opens, the neighbours get to know immediately. A motherly hand on my head gives way to a startling torrent of tears buried for long, that was just waiting to flow like an ocean. In all fairness to me, there are enough reasons to moan about and I have no qualms about turning into a sobbing mess for a while. I cry. I cry like a baby while sipping the homemade ginger chai. Mrs Srivastav fusses over me like a mother hen. Without knowing me, she seems to know everything about me. That I was a useless child to my parents when they needed me the most. She has all the right to presume so. It is absolutely her business to tell me about my karma. I was obsessed with fitting into some so-called lifestyle and achievement that did not matter now. 'I am here to change,' I convince

Mrs Srivastav, lowering my eyes. 'Trying to change,' I add. She understands but there is an undeniable look in her eyes, an unhappy look. I do not know her. And yet I feel she understands me in the absence of my mother.

I summon all my energy and ask about my father. Assuming she would know why the house is empty, but unfortunately, to my surprise, Mrs Srivastav only knows that the door has been closed for almost a month now. There is an extra set of keys with her. Shobha, the help who used to come to clean the house, also stopped coming a few weeks back. When probed a little further, she mentions some rumours that he is away somewhere in the mountains leading a monk's life. As soon as she blurts this out, she tries to backtrack and be diplomatic. She insists it is something she has overheard from her husband talking to other men, about his newfound life. She starts crying. 'Why are you crying, Aunty?' I ask her, confused.

My father did like a reclusive life. He was not very fond of socializing and hardly attended any parties. Amma had to follow him wherever he went. But attaining a life of a mendicant after her death was not something I can easily believe. He was so much in love with himself that there was no one he could think of apart from himself.

Mrs Srivastav smiles after the sudden burst of tears. There is a sense of peace to her that seems infectious. I am thinking of Amma and her at the same time. Their generation knew how to deal with complex emotions.

They were strong to witness the loss of their near ones. When Amma lost her mother at a young age, she must have suffered through many of the emotions I am now going through. She chose love with each passing year, accepting her reality and tried to live in harmony, despite the tempestuous nature of my father, who would suddenly burst into a fit of anger only to calm down in sometime. She chose to ignore her hurt, hoping it would bring her peace or perhaps she chose to complain for momentary relief, only to suffer through new pain.

I can keep frowning but now, having met Mrs Srivastav and learning a tiny life lesson, I must find a father who is absconding in the remaining journey of this cherry-picked life.

✧

The heat outside is normal for others but too much for me, I decide to dig into my mother's cupboard and investigate my father's too. I have this strong urge to know more about their story. There is still nothing to eat at home, but I delay this 'to-do list' for the afternoon stroll. This moment takes me back to Raga[20] Dhanashri reverberating in our house. Amma had a lot of South Indianness in her because of her father's posting for a brief period in the southern

---

[20]A traditional pattern of notes in Indian music

forest ranges. She picked up Tamil and understood Tamil TV shows that were as colourful as her crisp South cotton saris. There must have been a lot of hidden emotions too which she chose to keep to herself. I wonder what she really dreamed about. What did she really want in life apart from her daughter's well-being?

We hide behind the closet called the world. It opens to a lot of unsaid reality and confusion and we bury our emotions within ourselves because of fear. What will people say? What will our near and dear ones say? Worried more about the smallest changes that can affect a controlled life, we choose to ignore our true feelings, only for them to rise again and again in some form or another. My Amma must have been in this category and I am sure there are many more like her, making sacrifices. Sacrifices for the children. Sacrifices for the husband. Sacrifices for the parents. It's a chain reaction. Like the *'maut ka kua*[21]*'* where the man keeps riding the bike round and round for the thrill, to make the people watching him happy. There must be so much fear inside him and yet he must be doing this out of necessity. The necessity of money, but also, most of us don't reveal our true feelings for the necessity of peace.

The time is right with the music, the Thillana raga is a soprano at this moment, echoing my sentiment, a feeling coming from deep inside. I decide to throw it open to

---

[21] Well of death

myself first and then to the world. 'Don't tease me, life. Aren't my sorrows yours as well?' the verses of the raga said.

Do I really trust myself?

I open the cupboard to see some files with old photographs of my parents and my grandparents just lying there lifeless, like shirts hanging on a rope. I realize my attachment to these smiling faces dressed in saris. The age difference in their era was not too much between the mother and their daughters and sisters. So, they were likely to be friends than the relationship dictated by blood. I look at my parents' wedding pictures. There was a calmness within I think, as I recall the fight that existed the last time I saw them both together. I marvel at the patience to handle each other for more than thirty years. I wonder what her father—my Baba—must have told her while she was getting married. *This is your husband now for the rest of your life and after your death too, he will remain your husband.*

Did she ever talk to my father the way she spoke to her cousin sisters? What were their conversations like in the privacy of their bedroom? Did she trust him completely? For that matter, did he trust her enough to tell her his innermost feelings? In all the time I saw them, I always felt they had this silent relationship where both knew what the other wanted even before they spoke to each other. Was my mother's love so pure? She must have hated so many of my father's habits. But did that make Amma want to stay away from him?

I flip through more documents. A marriage certificate, and below it, a yellow wedding card written in English in brick red colour, marking a date in the 70s:

'Shubh Vivah'[22]

Sudha Awasti

Daughter of
{Mrs Sheela Awasti & Dr Mohan Awasti (IFS-Forest)}

with

Vishal Chaturvedi
{BA. MA. LLB. PhD (Archaeology)}

Son of
{Mrs Rama Chaturvedi & Ramanand Chaturvedi (IAS)}

According to the wedding card, only my father and grandfather were educated; no one bothered to print my mother's education. Amma had done MSc (Botany, Microbiology) and was a topper in her college. She was also a sports and dramatics enthusiast and the college president. But it did not matter. What mattered was the two families were worthy enough for an alliance. It did not matter if their personalities were not a match, did not matter whether their hearts were invested in the relationship.

---

[22] Auspicious wedding

This was what trust meant then. I remember my father's mother, Mrs Rama Chaturvedi; I used to call her Laddu, because every time I met her, she would ask whether I would like to eat a laddu. My mother was called Amu. I did not have a pet name myself. Amma's parents, after staying in almost all the forests, finally decided to settle down in the lush greens of the Himalayas. They found some land in a small town, the junction to the forests that was indescribably beautiful. My grandfather, who I called Baba, wanted a comfortable, non-chaotic life for his family amongst the flora and fauna. He was making way for my mother's dream to come true, a land where she could grow gifts from earth; but life had other plans. An unplanned marriage prospect came by which was so good that she walked into the land of discoveries with my father. Amma always believed that life would take her to where she belonged, but my father had no interest in living attuned to nature, belonging to a meticulous world where there was no room for daydreams.

My eyes fall on a crumpled piece of paper lying in the corner of the cupboard. A page from an old diary preserved for the ages, gibberish sentences in my father's handwriting which I cannot comprehend, marked with a date that correspond to my mother's demise months back. I had opened the cupboard on a whim trying to find clues to what inspired my father to leave home without informing a soul. I see some photographs fallen on the floor waiting to be picked. As I pick those photographs, a strange feeling rises, I have never seen these photos before and do not remember those moments.

Sepia-toned photos filled with nostalgia shows my grandfather with his only daughter, my mother standing on the ledge of a forest jeep at the entrance of a vast jungle. His expression is full of pride, like he has just won a war against jungle terrorism in his various postings. The Himalayan range was his last home, after which he settled in the northern mountains. My mother had lost her mother when she was nine, after which my grandfather and mother turned into two adventurers exploring the earth. As I see another happy face of a father and his 10-year-old daughter, standing on the steps to the holy Ganges, I feel as if a voice is beckoning me and it triggers something in me. I decide I must pack my bags and leave right away, following this photograph which tells me a story. With a bag pack filled with only essentials, a few pair of clothes. a photograph tucked in my book and a crumpled note in my pocket, I close the door of my temporary home behind me.

Which way to go?
I ask myself.
Track your memories.
They take you along.
The road has many turns

I will need to walk,
Follow my heart.
Which way to go?
I ask myself.

4

Standing at the ticket counter of the bus stop, I'm staring at the various faces of humankind. The faces, the skin texture, the language changes every hundred odd kilometres and it can take years for an anthropologist to understand even a slice of the ethnography of this beautiful country of divine beings. I stand at the small window staring at the board. The man at the counter automatically asks me, 'Just one ticket for Benaras?' I feel confused. Is this the universe trying to guide me with pit stops in different forms? 'Yes, just one ticket. I need a window, please?' I stammer in reply.

From the disappointment of not seeing my father and harbouring vague ideas of where he has disappeared, my thoughts, I realize, have become more perceptive to my surroundings. I take my seat in a not-so-crowded bus and look out the window. In a matter of minutes, the bus is groaning from the weight of gunny bags, some shoved on my side; from my seat I see legs dangling from the top of the bus. As it moves, I am trying to take in the beautiful surroundings that is going through rapid climatic as well as socio-economic changes; I am inching closer to the land of the oldest traditions. A part of me wants to follow the path of millions of pilgrims who are fascinated by the simple faith in the strange workings of the universe and are carrying various life experiences. Like them, I need the divine intervention of the invisible strength.

Not having a phone with an Indian sim card yet is one of the first signs that I am on the spiritual path of, to use the most overused words, 'finding myself'. Otherwise, by now, I would be only looking down at my screen beeping with messages and not outside the window. My fingers would have gone numb messaging and scrolling through the social media platforms which never fail to show the glittery lives of people. I would zero in on the next photograph that will be uploaded on my timeline. Then I would start phrasing my caption for the photo. Our life stories are photographed for social media. Where did we check in? What did we eat? Which restaurant did we go to? What does our bedside look like? Telling someone 'I love you' and that he is adorable on social media when he is sitting right next to you. The next day we might even break up. When I look back, it seems ridiculous. Right now, am I missing it? Yes, I am. But I am also thankful that I have still not had the urge to get a new sim. Although the urge to upload and share this travel kicks in, I am waiting to see how long I can abstain. The crowded bus is lumbering its way on the unstable roads. The twitch in my stomach comes back.

As I look out, the wind gives me a sweet little kiss. So many times I look up to the sky and just stare at it, even unknowingly; I am used to drawing patterns in the clouds. Sometimes, the sky looks like giant scoops of ice-cream. Sometimes, like a grandmother's white hair. Sometimes, like fluffy froth in a cup of coffee. Sometimes, like candyfloss. If you look hard enough, you can always find different imaginative faces in the shape of a cloud. We have a huge landscape in the sky to discover our own metaphoric stories. No one judges you when you stare at the sky. It legitimizes doing nothing and is a perfect antidote to a digital world where everyone is perpetually expanding their to-do lists.

I love to look at a clear sky and just stare, creating a pattern in my head in absolute stillness. The enchanting feeling of watching a cloud over you sometimes casting a shadow on a sunny morning is time spent well. The grey clouds cast a dark spell over you creating a pensive mood that makes you want to be alone with your thoughts. The same clouds touching the mountain, gliding in the hilly areas, creates an inward mood of wanting to be with yourself.

Like the clouds, my mind is also in transition.

5

The small winding steps in one of the old structures facing the ghat[23] takes me to Shanti Guest House which has a sign saying, 'Welcome All' written in English. I look at the hand-painted lotus flowers on the wall. A faint yellow bulb that is gathering dust throws its light to show me the way to a half-asleep man who looks like the caretaker working overtime. There is a bit of eeriness as he tells me, 'Madam, there is no single room available right now.' I wonder where I will stay at this hour of the night. 'I am okay to even sleep here on this sofa,' I say. He leaves the table asking me to wait. He comes back with a comforting smile and says, 'A shared room is available.' I ask, 'Who is in the room with me?' He stares at me with a yawn, 'A girl'.

---

[23] A flight of steps leading down to a river

I hardly had any white friends in America. I thought when you are among brown skin, you can truly be yourself. I wanted to be part of a larger unit, but I was scared of it too. With time, I realized people are the same everywhere, only the faces change. The thoughts, the sorrows, the laughter and the frowns are all the same.

I look at the Southeast Asian girl on the bed next to mine. She is sleeping peacefully. I am staring at the ceiling fan again. I was never a disciplined kid in school and always liked doing many things at once. The moment I had many sources for entertainment, my enthusiasm would be high for one of them for a while and then diminish as time went by. I used to dance but quickly got bored and left it. I went to the gym for a few days, got bored and left it too. I made friends very easily and then got bored of meeting them and ran out of things to say to them. Maybe it was the same with the boyfriends too, relationships that always remained unfinished.

Now the moment has arrived to follow each chakra, I have chosen to travel from the depth of the Muladhara Chakra—the first chakra located at the base of the spine to the Sahasrara Chakra—the seventh chakra located at the top of the head intending to heal every energy path. I don't know whether this cleansing map is going to work. But I know for sure that Amma would be very happy that, for once in life, I am making an attempt to have a clear path. I remember my mother's repeated warnings,

'Oorja, stop adding so much clutter to your life.' It's time to concentrate on what matters. Because the drama in my life will continue and I need to keep fixing it like a pipe leakage. I will start with buying a few salwar-kurtas. I stare at my boots; they are useless in this weather, I think to myself. Reaching the dead end of thoughts, my eyes close as I plonk on a soft pillow placed on a hard mattress.

∽

As an orange light passes through the window, my eyes open to an empty bed.

The girl is missing. I thought I would speak to her, make friends and we would stroll, discussing the oldest city in the world. But the Ganges is for solace as we submerge ourselves, reflecting on our past and emerge as a new person finding inner strength to move forward. The old is gone and I welcome the new which feels intensely spiritual now.

I step out to an ocean of people at the ghat, everyone vying for holy attention. Everywhere my head turns, I see holy men sitting still, mesmerizing curious minds in all colours, philosophizing about the higher values of life in fluent hindi and broken English. There are some of the rare sadhus[24] walking by, I've been told that you're not

---

[24]Saints

supposed to look into their eyes directly. If they catch you staring, there's a rippling effect in the body. I keep walking along, absorbing the colours and sounds, not wanting to step into the Ganges and purify myself. For now, I just want to be a food travel show host, discovering the right places to eat.

Walking on a road full of honking scooters, past rickshaws with men who stop to ask if I want to go a buy Benarasi sari or to a guest house. Cheap and clean places guaranteed. I say 'no' a couple of times. At the corner of a small lane, there are a bunch of people eagerly waiting to eat puri subji. I rush to join the so-called queue. I am very fond of the orange-yellow aloo rasaa[25], so I patiently wait my turn. A hand places a plate of puri sabji with extra puri on the side for me.

I finish my plate in a jiffy. The red powder is spreading a heat wave through my ears.

The boy asks me, 'Want more?' Before I can nod my head with my stuffed mouth, there's a jalebi[26] staring at me from my plate—the sugary dipped orange twirls asking me to take just one bite. Now here's a sweet that cannot be compared to any donut or cream cake in the world. How can anyone compete with this diversified culture? Overwhelmed with joy, I take one bite, then two and

---

[25] A thin curry
[26] An Indian sweetmeat

finally, the last piece of the jalebi, thinking about all the times Amma fed me piping hot jalebis adding sweetly, 'You won't become fat by eating just one more.'

A mother will always think her child is thin. They can see it in front of their eyes that their child is not in a good shape, but they still choose to ignore it. I was one of those kids. Not exactly obese, but definitely the Indian kind of 'healthy'. It took me a while to lose the weight. Actually, it was the preponderance of over-the-counter food that made me lose weight. Half the time, I threw it into the dustbin.

When I was here, I used to complain about the food my mother made. Sometimes, it was late. Sometimes, not the way I wanted it to be. My mother always abided my stupid pickiness about food. Along with my father's. There was not even one day where I did not see her preparing his food unless there was a serious emergency. Even if she was down with a cold or fever, his dabba[27] was made with clockwork precision. 'Don't eat outside, I will make it at home' was the imperative rule. It's surreal to see a person with the same routine every day for decades without an ounce of complaint. Even with the available online apps for food, if she was here, she would have told me, 'I can make it at home, beta. Why are you spending money?' After a few seconds, she would add with a quirky smile,

---

[27]Tiffin

'But we can spend all the money on our favourite chaat[28] when your father goes on tour.'

Unprompted, tears roll down my face when I remember how once there was family time, where everyone sat together and had a hearty laugh and meal. Now, it's mostly food out of a box for everyone, eaten in bed, with only our phones for company. They are our best friends. When we are sad, we go on social media and see how beautiful everyone's world is and then feel worse about ourselves. We try to make sure that our life is equally good, so a makeshift world is created to satisfy our own ego. Right now, I don't want to obsess over a virtual world. And I don't want it to know every detail of every minute of my life.

I walk through the narrow lanes with these thoughts buzzing in my head. While I am gallivanting, I see a man reading palms under an enormous tree.

Astrology can be your best friend when the stars have something nice to say while it can be a rude shock when the predictions are not as per your expectations. The horoscope for each sign printed daily in the newspaper has a very funny effect on us. How will our day go and what is in store for us? Whatever we read in the morning keeps flashing in our mind; if an event goes awry, we attribute it to a prediction, that is more a forewarning. What if we were to follow every instruction in the daily horoscope? There

---

[28] A savoury snack

would be chaos. We'd have to wear the colour recommended by the predictions. If, one day, it said, 'Take care of your money today', somewhere in the corner of our minds, we would worry about what we have read.

The palm reader with the dull grey face does not say anything but his silence says a lot as he peers at my hand without touching it. He looks at me and tells a story, 'You have found a new path and it's a reflection of the self. The road map is clear, the journey you have begun would make it imperative for you to shed the old and embrace the new.' He leaves me there standing still with his beautiful kohl-lined eyes compelling me with an unspoken command, 'Notice signs at every step.'

It is my hope that I am finally on my way to find what I am looking for. My father and I need to accept that there is no escaping the chaotic fabric of this journey. Vasco da Gama did it; he travelled from one corner of the world to discover new places. Buddhist monks travel for enlightenment. I am travelling as an explorer who will not be sent back, who will find a dialogue between the inside and outside and live nowhere and everywhere. Did I just say that? Have I decided to stay back?

Unaware of the passing time, I sit on the steps of the ghat merging into the river. The sun is changing its colours, from throwing a dark shadow to emitting light spreading like fire, staring at the flowing river, not worried about who these people are, the many who keep visiting her. All of them praying that their fears, their faults, their agony disappear with the dip in the river.

Often, we imagine that which is not actually there to be real. We fabricate situations according to our convenience and no matter the circumstance, we make sure that this is how the story should unfold. And when it is not like we have imagined, the pain, the anguish, the frustration, anxiety or tension builds up only to turn us into a shell of what we once were. Personally, I need a positive change to improve my life, to be at peace with things as they are. I am giving myself over. Changing myself to change a little of the world. I am far more than my thoughts, my past and the figments of my imagination.

With the fading light, I can see the silhouettes of boatmen getting ready to return home and another set getting ready for the evening shift. I step into a boat; the boatman welcomes me with a smile. Looking at my reflection with floating lamps in the water, I am flowing with her, my Amma.

Death has many reasons to arrive. Perhaps Amma had to go for me to arrive here. She was the teacher, the student and the lesson. I needed to return to my original untouched state of mind. I slip in and out of my imaginings, the faint sound of children practicing a raga, trickles into my ears. Would I have heard them if I wasn't floating on this tranquil water? My mind is less chaotic. The river seems to be bathed in light. There are ceremonies being conducted for loved ones who have left this world. A variety of sounds and sights fill my senses. The fragrance of incense. The fire spilling ash. The sound of the temple bells. They all have a story. Not my story. Not my thoughts, ideas or opinions.

Something special is happening. It is the voice in me being silent, being cognizant that the flow of the river takes its own course. I am coming to my senses. Could just stepping out of your comfort zone actually bring a change in you? I do not know the real reason of this sudden change of perspective. They say when you visit the Ganges, you need to give up something you really love. I am still trying to determine what I really love and want to give up forever. The one I loved has already left.

My emotions sweep me away. Smoking and anger have to be thrown into the Ganges.

Dark orange playing hide and seek with yellow, I see marigolds in bunches by the temple steps, these marigolds that can take your breath away. They are everywhere. In all kinds of occasions. During birth and death. As I stand in the queue to pay my respects to the Lord, I try to understand the reason why there are so many standing like me in this queue praying to the Almighty for His divine intervention. I stand looking at the faces around me, some with eyes closed. Some lips are muttering verses, mouthing prayers.

I want to experience this divinity that has people

entranced. When problems are solved and prayers are answered, they come here in gratitude. The power of the invisible force pushes me inside and here I am, in front of the divine. Something hits me. An energy so strong, combined with the chants, I stand still, and the earth seems to be whirling around me in the form of humans.

I am learning something new, an ingenious history of my roots. This is what Amma always did; she engaged herself fully in what she was doing without losing focus. When she was cooking, she was fully immersed in the act of cooking. When she was tending to my needs, she was a hundred per cent with me. The art of focus, to think of the present and not flit from one thing to the next was one of her traits. She was there for everyone when she was needed. Today, when we require constant affirmations—that we are good, that there is no fear of missing out, we have this compulsive need to be everywhere, and aware.

As humans, we were embodied with a higher consciousness that disregarded anything that caused discomfort to Mother Earth. Striving for the highest perfection is what I want to achieve, in my mind and through my actions. As I stand here amidst so many god-fearing humans, each with their own idea, I know with a certainty that God is around me. But I cannot depend on this invisible aura of the universe solely, I have to summon the force within me.

It has been almost a decade since I entered a holy

place. I always thought of myself as someone who leaned towards Pagan beliefs. Someone who felt that the Almighty was around us. In the trees. In human expressions. In the rivers and the seas. The feeling of having one source of energy up there who is looking at you. Even when you fail or do things that are not right, God is up there watching you, and also allows you to make mistakes, like I have, and then resurface from the beginning as if nothing has happened. Isn't this beautiful? Even in relationships, there are no second chances. In the world of constant gratification and immediate results, there is no space for I-made-a-mistake-but-I-can-rectify-it.

In the corporate world, you get one warning. Then perhaps another and then you are given an exit letter. There is no patience. Take online shopping, for that matter. Think of the OTP number which is sometimes a second late. When a car suddenly speeds before us, we are angry. The signals resound with terrible honks because we don't want to wait for it to turn green. The courier guy gets a piece of our mind because a book which was supposed to come in the morning came in the evening. As if we were going to read this book on the spot and finish it! The door does not open after three bells and we want to break the door. But what about the appointments we are late for? That does not have any justification. Our impatience takes over us and in minutes, we are anxious. In a split second, a person collapses without any perceivable reason.

A normal conversation turns into an ugly fight. A flock of birds fly upon hearing a loud sound. A crash inside a car. Like Amma. In that moment, there are no second chances.

Here I am getting a second chance.

I am curious about the afterlife. Death happens. It is an inevitable part of our lives. There is a pattern and when the time comes, everyone has to go. I have always imagined what it must feel like to have the one you love in your arms as they take their final breath. One moment, she was talking to you and the next there are so many things left unsaid. A silence that only whispers through the soul. Can the departed soul still hear us? Is it true that even as our heart stops beating, there is a sense of aliveness and our whole life flashes before us in a fraction of a second?

The smoke from a nearby fire envelops the sky; I look in the direction it's coming from and see a bright yellow flame which highlights the humans performing the last rites of a loved one. All on the same ghat, praying for the deceased. Some accept the fact. Some take some time for the truth to sink in. As I watch them from this side of the ghat, I feel a connection with my mother. I feel as if she is around and is trying to seek my attention. We still have a lot to talk. Does she speak to me? Yes, she does, otherwise I would not be here. I am only following her path. I keep turning over the crumpled page in my hand. Trying to decipher my father's cryptic writing.

I notice my roommate sitting next to me and I smile

at her. She smiles back but does not reciprocate with any word; we both know we share the same room. There is this strange kinship between us. She looks at the smoke from the fire lighting up in the darkness. I follow her eyes and see the blazing fire calling out to me.

I unknowingly walk towards it into the river as it keeps coming closer to me, the heat binds me with Amma's warmth. *'My ashes with yours into the river of eternity, until we meet again, o dear one,'* my father's words meld with it.

A rush of tears flow from my eyes with the beat of a pounding heart. I call out for my roommate. The steps on the ghat are empty. Is she real? I cry looking at the reflection of the passing clouds. My trembling legs in the cold water on this dark evening keep reminding me that Amma is around, protecting me and I am fulfilling her wish. Did my father sit on the same steps and brood under the same sky? As I turn, carrying a silent fire within me, the astrologer is looking at me as he walks past. His eyes remind me to look at the signs. I steps at him walking into the holy waters and merging into the darkness.

PART 2

6

There are voices that need to be heard.
Voices that are silent.
Voices that reflect thinking.
Of the heart that burns.
Of fear of thorns.
A sound of ifs and buts.
It seems a break from infinity.
This may end.
This may not.
There is still a beginning.

The clouds seem to be floating so close, they might as well be inside the bus. Outside, the mountains stand tall as the colours of the sky change according to the mood of the sun. The Palash trees emit an orange red glow filtering through the green leaves, making it violet. The leaves of the trees swaying with the dense fog release a strange fragrance.

My mind is quiet, asking me to stop, take a deep breath and let go. The evergreen dark wood Chir Pine with cones waiting to fall, the branches with pointed leaves feel like they are crouching to offer a hug. With every season, they shed their old self, bringing in newness.

We often cannot choose who travels with us. The person who sits beside you in a bus or plane or train can make all the difference, especially if you are travelling alone. A handsome companion for a long ride can be a most pleasant surprise. When the bus driver takes a sudden turn, the sides of your shoulder brush his with a little smile. The little pleasures of that moment. The journey will end with a 'see you' or a 'bye'. There is a difference. The difference between exchanging numbers with the promise of meeting again in the future as opposed to never seeing each other again. I am hoping that this little fantasy would be met in the bus. Because the last bus ride and the plane journey did not reward me with a seat partner. The seat beside me has been empty for too long. With every halt, I peep out of the window to see if there is anyone special. Women, busy with the rigours of everyday, are taking a routine journey different from mine.

The wind forcefully closes my eyes, taking me back to a holiday where I had escaped with my mother, to a mosaic of plantations with a forest and grassland, inhabited by several endangered species. The thought of those times we spent among nature forever evokes special memories.

Mapping Love

It was those rare moments of family time together when even my usually taciturn, monosyllabic father would ask me about school, enquire after my studies. I wish he had told me stories. I look at the crumpled paper once again, unfolding the creases on the words that don't mean anything to me. I always looked up to my mother for that comfort. Amma was indeed a mother tree, who provided support by giving nutrients to those withering around her but try as you might, sometimes a fallen tree cannot be held back together again and when the roots go weak, she falls. I am like the withering tree who is not strong enough to stand on her own.

I saw this fall in the last relationship which feels almost surreal now. We had met at a hair salon, both of us had been double booked with the same stylist. I like getting my hair cut by men. They treat you well and there is 'bro-hood'. They tell stories while snipping, stories of far-off lands. Of how they miss their family. I feel like one of them. After the haircut, they become friends. A haircut appointment is actually two friends sharing home-grown secrets that stay inside the salon. He was waiting and so was I. We said a tentative hello and then both of us were okay with either of us going first and waiting for the other. I insisted that he should get his haircut first. I could wait since I anyway had to catch up with Soyu, my South Asian stylist. He started getting his hair done while I stood there. He asked for my opinion. He was simple. A middle-class Indian boy with a slight accent. I tried giving answers as well as suggestions. 'This short hair with a little spike looks like my favourite Hollywood actor,' I said. He was the kind of men I like immediately. Soyu added masala[29] to the conversation by adding more appreciation for his haircut.

He waited for me as I got my hair done. I saw him standing in the corner like a Texan hero from a Western classic. I went and stood next to him like a bystander enjoying my new haircut. Without any drama and not waiting for me to ask for his cigarette, he shared his last one with me.

'This haircut behaves exactly like you.'

I did not know what he meant. He gave me a pointed stare while I took my time to reply. There was silence and then he abruptly said, 'Let's have dinner'. Both of us had nothing to do in New York City but relished the freedom that comes with losing oneself in the crowd.

I had not asked his name.

He had not asked mine.

I slipped.

Oorja.

Vikrant.

Smiles were exchanged once again.

After many relationships which could be categorized as 'friends with benefits', this one felt like I was coming

---

[29]Spice

to the surface to take big gulps of air after drowning for a while.

'Have you ever thought of going back home?' he asked.

I immediately said, 'No'. He was a little taken aback and there was silence for a second. I still don't know why we were suddenly so awkward with each other. He reached over and pulled a strand of hair off my face. An electric wave passed through my spine and I wanted to kiss him right there. He was deliberately taking it easy, both of us savouring our Italian meal with a glass of wine.

The dinner was a fairly elaborate meal. I stood outside the restaurant with him as his face shone on a night that was as bright as the glow signs. My after-meal cigarette was almost over and I was getting a little anxious about the next step. Both of us had to leave in the opposite direction when he broke my chain of thought, 'Are you taking the train or the cab up to your house?' 'I am taking neither,' I said, stubbing the last one of the day. I was going to walk and relish going over our dinner and conversation. For once, I was not thinking of going to bed with this man. 'Will you walk along with me?' I asked him with a longing look in my eyes. Without saying a word, we walked under an aubergine sky among lush greens, with flowers strewn on our path as gushes of wind brushed the tiny petals.

I kissed him first.

He reciprocated.

I felt like a leafy tree touched by the breeze.

Silent in the chaos of New York, we walk past neon lights flashing on confused faces, hurriedly walking on the streets. Our shoulders caressed each other, his hand around mine, we walked under the stars which felt like thousands of fireflies illuminating a dark night, bringing meaning to a number of questions I never wanted to know the answer to.

I followed the rhythm of his footsteps.

He wrapped his arms around me with such cozy warmth that it could have put me to sleep. His lips tasted of a cinnamon stick waiting to be had.

Neither of us spoke.

The long walk ended in his apartment. I lay on the bed as he engulfed me with his illuminating gaze. I was ready to be his as we both let each other in, without a second thought.

A voluptuous night of passion ensued, and I opened my eyes to the morning rays sparkling on the bedsheet which filled me with the images of the night before. We were beside each other with desire.

I remember wondering if it was real.

He got up to get ready for work. 'You can take your time, stay here if you like for a while.' With his glasses and smart casuals on, he looked bright in the morning light.

No number left.

No trace of who he was.

I decided not to leave. Maybe he knew I would stay and maybe he knew that there would be another long night. Maybe he assumed that I was between jobs. Maybe I was thinking too much.

For a man, and presumably a bachelor, the huge studio apartment was well kept. There were loads of newspapers lying around. I made myself a cup of black coffee and sat by the table with a book called, *Seeking Everyday Happiness*. His smell still lingered. I was distracted and needed some sleep.

A touch.

The sunrise had turned into sunset. I was in deep slumber when his breath woke me up.

He smiled and gave me a cup of coffee.

I had wondered if it was real. 'You are real,' he said to me.

'Why did you ask me to stay back?'

'You trusted me, and this somehow feels momentous.'

I had not been in a real relationship and smiled at his perceptiveness. He was nowhere close to my age but that did not matter. He lived in one of the best cities in the world; he had a steady income and a studio apartment. More than anything, he seemed all that is good and decent.

Days blurred into weeks and months. The evenings were better. He took care of me like I was the only one he had on his mind. I continued doing research, looking for my next job. He never bothered to check with me about my work. Whenever we spoke, it was only about the house. He asked me a couple of times about the idea of marriage. I had no clear answer. Marriage was never on my mind. The long dinners consisted of him telling me about his family back home. How they had really worked hard to get him there. How they had given up their own ambitions for him to succeed. He missed them most of the time. I felt like sinking sand getting sucked into his life. After a while, he expected me to be home when he returned from work, ready with the table set. He ate wholeheartedly, not looking at me even once while I sat in front of him waiting for him to ask me about my day. He never asked me about my plans for finding a job. I had given up my apartment and moved in with a man who, as it turned out, wanted someone at his beck and call.

There were days of abrupt anger and the nights were reserved for dominant sexual play which had become a habit and did not feel sensuous anymore.

He refused to use protection.

I am pregnant
Give it up.
We don't need one so soon.
A hard slap on my face.
Tears rolling.
Don't you know how to protect yourself?
Another slap.

Mapping Love

In the blinding nights, tears would roll down my cheeks as the man of the house slept with calm-faced arrogance as if nothing was amiss. I was not allowed to step out without his permission. The house keys were not with me. I was locked inside. My phone was taken from me. There were many times I begged for him to return my phone. But he called me a loner, so why did I even need a phone? He did not like me talking to anyone. He caught me once on the phone in the bathroom. I was beaten and pushed to the edge of the bathtub. My throbbing head split open and I lay there unconscious.

I opened my eyes to see a couple of cops. I was told V was under therapy. I was not the first woman to get embroiled in his web of love, lust and anguish. I had a sudden flashback of the papers I had once found in his bookshelf. I acknowledged them as his research papers. The notes of wisdom in his cupboard. The messages on his phone. The frequent changing of passwords. He was helplessly trying to recover. The man I fell in love with walked along with me for what felt like an interminably long and disturbing time. Frail and angry, I stepped out into the sunlight waiting for me. I switched on my phone. Staring at it for some time, I called Amma. She was not there to pick up the pieces of my despair in the middle of a busy street on a New York afternoon.

I cried. I cried. I cried.

I forgave.

7

I stumble into the present as the bus stops for a loo break. I get down to stretch myself, looking out at the huge coniferous trees. The rhododendrons are not in bloom, but the fragrance of pine and fresh air has a soothing effect. Would I see him again? What if he emails me? Would I reply? What if he is sick? What if he is no more? There are many ifs and buts. On that one day, life took a turning point on a busy junction of America where everyone who passed by were so busy that they ignored a cry for help. Flying home had a new meaning this time—to find my mental stability and get over the events that had left a scar deep inside me.

The final stop is a little town near Corbett National Park. A long straight road leading to the jungle has many small hand-painted boards of forest lodges with phone numbers and 'clean stay' written in bold. The taxi drivers, waiting to fill in their seats, run towards the bus to catch hold of their potential customers, each screaming a different destination. The pre-booked forest jeeps are waiting patiently for their turn as passengers find their way. Seeing those jeeps, my mood turns nostalgic, remembering my genius grandfather welcoming me to his abode with a glint in his eye. Every time we went for a forest visit, even if the roads were the same, there was a new experience he created. He filled our lives with new experiences in a part of the world where life is slow. He existed within the reach of civilization and was still aloof but always happy. Being around him, my heart was happy.

I am looking at the visitors, government officials and locals around me and reminiscing about the days spent with my grandfather. A registered driver of the jeep comes to me and asks me, 'Do you have the parchi?' The receipt. I look at him suspiciously when he directs my eyes to the badge he is wearing on the right of his uniform. I sheepishly open my bag and dig deep into my wallet to find the folded print-out from the website. I am depending on paper and asking people for directions. When the world is going digital, I am detoxing. He reads the fine print and asks me for any sort of identification. Once more, my fingers fish out my passport. He looks at my photo and then back at me. I look much younger in my passport picture, with longer hair, heavy on the face. He takes my passport and shows it to another driver who looks like his senior. His head turns towards me too. I am nervous when I have no reason to be. I have already paid online with my international card for the two nights I am going to spend here. They do not seem to trust me. The driver comes back with my passport and says, 'The name on the passport is different from the one in the receipt. But your face looks the same.' I sigh as I look at the document. I had spelt my name wrong in a hurry to finish filling the form. I had written Oorja haphazardly, so much so that even I cannot understand my handwriting. He allows me to get inside the jeep with a warning that I should be clearer in my documentation.

The jeep starts. I am sitting at the back with my rucksack. A bearded man who looks like a writer and a middle-aged guy dressed in a pair of camouflage pants and a khaki shirt sits in front. A serious photographer, perhaps? The one in the front looks like office staff who has files in an off-white canvas bag. He talks about how saab[30] wants to spend a few days at the lodge. It is a déjà vu moment for me sitting in the same place. I am the only woman. No one is bothered about my presence. I perhaps look like another hippie, travelling alone to the mountains to find meaning in my life. The ones you should ignore because they cannot be conversation starters unless you need a cigarette. I have forgotten what smoking feels like

---

[30]Sir

until I glimpse a few hands sharing a beedi[31], finishing their last one before they start the jeep. Strangely, it does not affect me.

The winding roads curl through the forest. The jeep looks tiny against the tall trees overshadowing us. As I look out, everything is vanishing in the rear-view mirror. The trees making sounds in the breeze, the occasional chattering birds, the sound of a passing train somewhere fill my senses. The officer who is sitting upfront is talking continuously and after some time, even his voice sounds like the buzzing of an insect in this vast array of biodiversity.

My mind wanders again to my grandfather who served most of his life in the wilderness this side of the country, among fresh tea leaves and immense greenery. The sound of birds mating is a common phenomenon here. In cities, the honking of vehicles is a part of your life. Here, it is the sound of a Bulbul singing a song of happiness, Sunbirds gathering twigs for their little nests, Woodpeckers aggressively hitting their beaks against the barks of trees which sway in the wind. Black and white photographs adorned the walls of his home, revealing his love for flora and fauna. The pride he took in naming the tigers at the reserve made us feel like they were his children.

We reach the forest guesthouse which is still exactly where it was years back. The wild creepers, along with

---

[31] A local cigarette

the friendly lizards, adorn the walls. I am greeted by the old, screechy wooden doors and musty smell of old times.

Apart from the staff of about four, there is hardly anyone else around in this place. I am still standing in the reception area, waiting to be told what to do next. No one comes by until I go and stand beside an old fragile face in a forest service's uniform and directly ask for 'Room no 3', stopping to add, 'in the old forest rest house.' He holds a bunch of bronze keys in his hand which he keeps turning to see which is number three. The lines on his face seem to hold many stories. He has done this every day of his life, welcoming new visitors of all ages and sizes. I am still waiting for him to say something. He then asks me, 'Passport?' His face is devoid of expression. I give him my passport and he looks at it carefully. Finally, there is a smile, as if we have known each other for a long time. The keys for room no 3 are in my hand. I drag my bag through the old alley, crossing a hall with a red floral sofa and cream-coloured curtains. I skip the early buffet dinner. The *aalu ki sabji* and onions are spreading their aroma. Guests are having their early dinner and talking about the prospects of 'sighting'. I have already registered for the morning safari, so there are no more bookings that I need to make.

I have a strange relationship with new places. I cannot sleep on the first night. I look under the bed to see whether there is anyone hiding there, waiting to pounce on me.

There are mysterious thoughts which grow in my head and only fade when I see a little light passing through the space below the door.

I am imagining what Vikrant must have felt about me. He destroyed my self-confidence, slowly, carefully. He had a psychological effect on me. Now to think of it, he told me a different story and then one story became a serious turning point in my life, compelling me to make a choice between him and my well-being. As I sleep in the room, a wooden cot with a deer head is looking at me, just as the night cricket sings.

'I feel tomorrow looks brighter. I feel tomorrow looks brighter.'

∫

The sun is waiting to rise. I'm standing on the banks of a peaceful river. A river gives so much love, from children launching their paper boats to quenching the dry throats of the thirsty. A stream of water is a sight, so still even when it is moving. The jungle guest house is not very far from the main entrance to the jungle. The sun is still hiding. Patience is the word in the forest. I stand there impatiently, wanting to get the first seat in the jeep. The view is better up front and a chat with the driver often reveals many hidden stories of the land. I do not have my camera. I have left it at home. Although I don't know which place to call home.

In the forest, animals are the king. Human beings are simply pawns. I feel like one even in the human world, a pawn who had given up everything she was passionate about, for a man. Perhaps, even more than love, I expected a little respect but when you are in love, your little world seems to be the whole universe and you have a myopic vision that is restricted to just the two of you. Maybe you even start losing your identity and live for the man who has no love for your ambitions.

What you were yesterday, you are not necessarily the same today. And what you are today, you may not be tomorrow. What is there is now, the precious now. This moment. A moment of living in this world, absolutely unfettered, like the song that you sing unprompted when you are happy, and you clap your hands. I clap with joy.

The driver interrupted, 'Keep your voice down, please!

As we drive deeper into the jungle, the tall trees rumble in the wind, communicating in the language only nature understands. I look up, thinking about the stories of powerful spirits that supposedly live in trees. In the Jataka tales, there is a story about an elephant who loved a particular tree; every time she felt afraid, she would take solace under the tree. One day, the elephant was rattling the tree in anger. It wanted the tree to support her. That day, the tree could no longer stay silent, it whispered words in the elephant's ears, 'Do you fear the wind? It only moves the cloud and dries the dew. Look inside your mind. There, fear alone has captured you'. This line about fearing the wind speaks to me too. I want to be peaceful like the grey blue sky which passes as moving images. I take a peek at the immense blue through the veil of the big leaves and the tall branches of infinite Sal trees.

The jungle is mysterious, and there are rules that everyone has to follow, even the most adamant creatures. It teaches you how to make your way through difficult situations. You have to follow a discipline that allows you to only keep moving forward. As an outsider, the forest is not your friend. But it is a teacher who can be difficult if you trouble her by not allowing her to breathe.

I spot a herd of deer basking in the morning sun. Sal trees also like to live in a group. They grow in groups. If one Sal tree grows alone, sadness eventually envelops her, and she ends up uprooting herself.

Man is a social animal. To isolate oneself from thinking, staying silent in absolute terms is a form of meditation to understand oneself. But being alone when you want to be among company, talking to yourself because you have no one to hear you, brings about a withdrawal of the self. The absence of a reliable partner creates loneliness in humans.

The langurs jump from one tree to another, keeping their eyes on the lookout for any trouble. A beautiful shaft of sunlight pierces through the thick foliage. The dark greens throw a wave of dusty yellow. A herd of elephants come into view and we stop at a safe distance to let them cross the road. The sight of an elephant couple and their little babies is an overwhelming reminder of the essence of relationships. It does not matter if you are a human or an animal, the bond between a parent and child is the same. The lioness hunts for her children while the lion father stays at home. The male sea horse creates a pouch for its child while the female works to get her child food. The male and female birds make nests together and they take turns to keep a check on their baby. This is the Yin-Yang philosophy of man and woman, two divided personalities that make one. Then why did Amma become a martyr of responsibilities while my father's every need became a command? If it can happen in the animal world, why is the human world so different?

One summer, when I was about fourteen, Amma wanted to come here and spend the holidays with her father. After months of planning and making sure that everything was in order, she finally told my father that she wanted to go and meet her father. Asking permission to meet your own blood seems odd, doesn't it? Strangely, I still vividly remember that night.

'How many days are you planning to go for?'

'I was thinking, for a month.'

In her mind, she'd already decided it would be about 45 days. She intended to call later and say that she would be extending her stay.

'Isn't that a bit too long? You are aware that I don't

eat food cooked by anyone else.'

That's sweet, my mother must have thought.

Except that wasn't what she was thinking. She was thinking about how I would study better and benefit from the stay with my grandfather.

Amma had planned for every eventuality and question that could be asked. My classes had already been fixed at the local government school that my grandfather supported. Anyhow, the night continued with even more questions. Some angry ones too. The forest survived on the game of instinct. If you have a strong mind, you can challenge the opponent and create your own space. Amma always had that foresight.

'I will go for ten days. Since you are going on a tour, what will I do sitting here? When you are back in a month or so, I will be back too,' she said, with a smirk on her face.

'Yes. I don't think you should stay here alone when I am not around,' my father reluctantly agreed.

At that time, my father was posted in the barren lands of central India for an important investigation of fossils that might conclusively prove that Dinosaurs existed there.

Mother knew his tour would have lasted ten days.

To push a man is stupid. To get your way through as if it was his idea is intelligence.

A tiger has crept up to the road right in front of our jeep. My heart is racing. It refuses to move and everyone around seems excited. Then there are the trained photographers and journalists, with long lenses and serious faces, resentful of people like us. The tiger has an ego that might surpass my father's spurts of tantrum.

You have come to see me, you jokers. He growls.

The area is surrounded by lush green foliage as everyone in their jeeps wait quietly to see the majestic tiger sitting in the middle of the road when in a split second, he gets up and disappears into the wild tall shrubberies without a trace. I voice the tiger's thoughts, 'When I feel like leaving I will, and you will keep moving around the jungle to spot me. But I will have the choice of not wanting to meet you.'

Animals are territorial. And so are new-age humans. The way Amma adjusted to my father's demands, whether it was how many teaspoons of sugar to be put in his tea or the shade of brown (*not dark brown but ochre brown*) he preferred. The food should be just about warm. Maybe he should have married a hotel. Better still, a robot. My mother adjusted to everything for a man who was convinced that only his way was right.

From my mother, I learnt the extent to which nature provides for us. Growing up in the forest, Amma realized very early, that nature has a way of telling us stories about various lives. About trials and turbulences. About giving and receiving. About living and letting others live. About day and night. About the moods it brings in. About being still and just letting go. About staying in the present as if there is no tomorrow.

8

I wake up in the middle of the night in room no 3 of the forest guest house and look at the crumpled paper with my father's handwritten lines. After the first two lines, I want to decipher the meaning of the next line, thinking perhaps it will help me look for the signs. I try to join the words to form a sentence, but his thoughts are written so rapidly that only he could understand, alongside Amma's date of demise which I can read clearly.

I am restless and get up to go to the reception. The old man is sleeping on a cot, his mobile phone kept on the edge of a side table. The mobile network does not catch here, and landline phone is the only way to connect. I pick one of the three numbers on the guest house visiting card and dial randomly. The second landline phone rings on the other side. In the stillness of the night, I can hear the phone ring echoing loudly. The old man is whistling as he snores. Obviously, no one is going to answer the phone at this hour. But I am happy that it is ringing. It's as if I am cracking a code now. I dial the next number just for the heck of it. And then a voice says, 'Hello, who is it?' It is authoritative. I immediately bang the receiver down, but it falls off the dial, with only for the incessant 'line is busy' sound to spread and reach the ears of the old man who wakes up. I leave the phone hanging through the wire and run into the room to lock the door behind me. I plonk myself on the bed and laugh loudly covering my face with a white pillow. Before I know it, my laughter turns to sobbing and again to laughter, then to a full-throated cry. I cry and laugh till my heart feels lighter. What am I doing here in the middle of the jungle? What is my destination?

I drift off to sleep until my eyes open to the knocking sound of the door in the morning.

The old man is standing with a register in his hands.

He asks me, 'Oorja Chaturvedi?'

I nod my head.

He has seen my ID and my name when I checked in; why was he asking me again? Also, why is he not asking me about last night? The phone calls. The disturbance I created in the middle of the night.

'Your check-out is today. You will have to vacate the room soon,' he says.

'Oh ok. Thank you,' I reply.

'Also, would you like to have lunch here?'
I immediately say, 'Yes'.
He goes back to being expressionless. I am waiting for him to ask me about last night, but he says nothing. It was a dream that has been forgotten in the daylight.

⌣

Later in the afternoon, I deliberately go to have lunch late so I can get a word in with the crotchety old uncle. I have to go to my grandfather's house where my mother had grown up before she got married and there is no way I can find my way without the help of some known old faces.

Alok Singh is old enough to know my grandfather. I sit beside him and try making conversation. Here, friendship happens over a cup of chai. You leave knowing the person's life history to visit him back, this time at home for delicious food and are even introduced as his best friend. I do not make any small talk. Without thinking of the consequence, I begin a round of rapid-fire questions.

'Did you know Dr Mohan Awasti?'

Hearing his name, the old man's ears expand like an elephant's.

'Do you know him?'
'Who are you?'
'His granddaughter.'
'You don't look like it.'

'Yes, I know but what do you need to know for me to prove that I am his daughter Sudha's daughter?

I inch closer to him. I stare him down.

'See my eyes. Same.'

I show the pointed nose which is a trademark of my maternal family. They take pride in it. Alok Singh is a no-nonsense man who does not speak more than ten words. His smile is instant, and he is the key to finding my lost father.

Alok Singh does not know much about my father but he used to work with my grandfather and knows enough about him. In small places, especially government quarters, the staff becomes a part of the Saab's family. Even though they are not related, they know everything about him. He fondly talks about Amma, rarely mentioning my father. All he says is that he has seen a few pictures of him with my mother in my grandfather's house. I pester him to take me to the house. I don't care what condition it is in; I just want to visit that familiar place from my childhood.

Alok Singh finds me strange, I can tell. How can a child not communicate with her father for so many years? Does anger bring anyone to a place where the whole world shatters and all that remains is a hand-written note of no consequence? How can a child not attend her mother's funeral? His words and look are enough for me coil myself into a ball of guilt.

He agrees to take the remaining day off. He tells me

that the least he could do is to help a lost child find her family house. By the time we leave, the whole guest house knows why I am here. Not to spot the animals, but visit my grandfather. Alok Singh yells when we talk, and it is as good as an announcement. That I do not have the number of my grandfather's house. That I did not attend my mother's funeral. Also that, I have not spoken to my father for months.

Driving the forest jeep on the long winding road, Alok Singh speaks faster than the wind. Suddenly, I cannot get the man, who has been so sullen and silent all this time, to stop talking. I let him speak his heart out. He says the same thing over and over again. He curses the influence of Western culture and upbringing. He talks about how so many youngsters are finding greener pastures overseas and how he has not gone out of the country even once. He wonders aloud whether the skyscrapers of America are actually real and if people really live on the 45th floor. I am patient because he is indirectly chiding me and I take it as verbal punishment. So what if he is a stranger?

'I wanted to tell you before when you asked about Awasti Sir.'

'What?' I ask.

'Do you know your grandfather is no more?' He finally said it, his voice heavy with emotion.

'What? Not at all. I was not there. I was studying in America. But why did you take so long to tell me?'

'Just felt it was not right.'

'Not right? What is wrong?' Perhaps that's why everyone is staring at me. I look away from him, wanting to go back.

'Do you want to turn back?'

'No, no. I want to go to my grandfather's house.' I have changed my mind.

'That does not answer my question.'

'My mother never told me,' I say as I feel my stomach churn once again, when I am tensed.

Silence.

'Do you know I found out that your mother also could not come?'

Silence.

'He died all alone. In his sleep.'

'Why did my mother not go?' I cannot help but think.

'Did she visit later?'

I look at him. His fragile eyes have seen many deaths. He seems to be waiting for his own.

'You did not meet her for many years?' It is like another punch to my gut.

My guilty eyes avert his.

As we drive, I try to think if the line in the verse on the note signals danger. I have dramatic thoughts lingering in my head: what if he has lost his memory? I remember Amma once saying that he had started forgetting things and even hallucinated sometimes that he was on a train going for an expedition with his colleagues.

Alok stops at a couple of places to greet the locals, then repeating 'Dr Mohan' like it is a chant. I am hoping to reach the house soon. For reasons known only to him, he goes through various lanes, even stops at a house while I sit inside the jeep waiting for him. He walks back and I see a boy holding a sack of potatoes for him come after him. After taking numerous turns, reversing with the brown dust blowing in my face and loads of sneezing, he stops a young woman with books in her hand, walking the muddy slush road, and asks her about her parents. I am really bored now; he has her full attention while I am left confused. There are no breaks after that, thankfully and we pass houses that look similar until we reach one that is standing tall at the end of the village and I feel as if it is someplace special.

It is almost dusk. The birds are wrapping up their exploring for the day and moving to their nests. The orange coriander rays of the setting sun dribble through the trees. I am standing in front of a stone house as old as me, covered in the shadow of welcoming trees. In front of me, there is a hand-painted sign. It reads,

> SUDHA GUEST HOUSE
> Only for female students
> IFS, MSC, PHD (Biology)

I can hardly stand without stumbling, as tears dampen my eyes. With my head bent, I cry for the trees to hear. For the birds to flutter away. For my mind to calm down.

A gentleman as old as Alok Singh stands authoritatively in front of me. He looks like my grandfather's friend, confidante, Man Friday and family. The only one I assume who was beside his deathbed. I stand up, clear my nose and gather myself. I walk quietly behind him like a schoolgirl without uttering a word. I enter the house and sink into a sofa which makes me look even smaller as I feel his eyes boring into mine.

I assume he would ask me difficult questions, judge me for the lifetime of suffering I have given to my mother and the family. My bags are taken inside, and I am asked to follow. The rooms have the fragrance of memories that have stayed inside, waiting for me, reminding me to ask for forgiveness. In the years she spent before her wedding and then after, she visited her father every chance she got. This was home for her. The permanent one. With her husband she had many homes, for every time he had a transfer, she would move with him to a new place. The houses never smelled of warmth. She had to pack and unpack time and again to lose her own identity. Each time, new friends had to be made. The old ones cast off. She could never call any of these homes hers. The Lucknow house was bought just a few years before she died.

How do you call something your own when you never

owned it? I have always wondered what happens to kids like me who never stay in one place for too long. Just when we are trying to make a house into our home, we have to shift to another. The friends are gone. The home is gone too. A house can never be a home unless you own it and absorb every brick of it like it's yours. Your stories stay in a home for generations.

I am guided to my room as I walk, the golden library, my grandfather's library that feels as if it was just built yesterday converses with me. The books you read, stay with you and come handy at a time when you have no one to speak to. It's a conversation starter. Like the one I had with Vikrant. He was impressed with my knowledge of books. My love for reading was majorly influenced by my grandfather and Amma. Every time we would go to meet him, my mother would carry a few books along with her for the road. Growing up, I had often caught her napping with a book in hand. Four-in-one digests. Detective series. Philosophy books. Worn out books on Botany which had dried leaves and flowers pressed between the pages or books on Indian culture or geography. Home gardening. How to grow herbs. The forests. The land. The sea. Without stepping out to explore, a whole world of knowledge was available in her little room.

Every time we had to move to a new house after my father got transferred, my mother would silently bear the verbal abuses of my father for packing so many kilos of books. The houses were always a surprise, sometimes we would get a big government house with four rooms and a nice garden and at other times, the quarters were small. Wherever my mom went, her cartons of books followed her. By the time we shifted to the last house before I left for America, Amma was getting tired and age was catching up. The cartons remained unopened. Most of them lay in the corner of a storeroom, some under the bed. The botany, organic gardening book was opened sometimes and referred to. With time, that habit too faded. My mother had lost interest in almost everything she loved. The gap between me and her increased like distances on maps but the phone calls never lessened. When I was in trouble, I called my rescue number.

Every time I think of my mother,
I see the shadow of an unsaid story.
Some things reveal themselves. Some do not.
Where was the gap?
She spoke. Did I hear?
Upset. A thousand words echoed.
She quietly heard them all.
There is nothing to worry,
My dear one.
The stars give light.
I am looking at you.
Your dreams.

Let them come. Let them go.
My sweet little child.
Sleep.

I close a book of poems upon hearing a voice behind me.

I turn to see Alok Singh standing in front of me.

My face changes in seconds as my eyes shift to the corner of the room.

A fragile figure in a wheelchair with no expression remains silent. I cannot gauge the situation for a few minutes. Everything is quiet except the wind making sounds brushing against the trees. On the wheelchair is my grandfather and he looks lost. Tears stream down my face unbeckoned. I must have done something right in the last few days to receive such an unexpected blessing.

It must have been so hard for a father to see his daughter go to heaven before him. Alok Singh had played a trick on me, taking advantage of my oblivious state. He knew how my grandfather was, but he played along with my disconnected side and made me aware of my weakness.

Whatever happened, happened for good. Whatever is happening is happening for good. Whatever will happen will also happen for good. We do not need to have any regrets for the past. We do not need to worry about the future. The present is happening. Live the present, says the Bhagwad Gita.

I begin again.

9

Baba stares at me for a long time. I find it difficult to express the words building up in my heart. I keep my guilt aside and go and sit beside him. He looks like the setting sun, beautiful but sad. I am about to say something when the person standing beside the wheelchair angrily says, 'He hardly speaks in syllables and can barely hear now. The whole family abandoned him, including his own son-in-law. This is not what he would have asked for. Do you see his state? Daughter had to go. But the granddaughter was even worse. She has not come to visit him even once. Went to Amerika!'

I am his granddaughter, but he can no longer recognize me.

The man said enough, there is a lot happening for me to reply.

This is one of life's most ironic moments. Here is

someone who could easily identify a tiger, various plants, could tell the age of a banyan merely by looking at it—a veritable forest encyclopedia. I feel uneasy as he just stares at me, unable to make sense of who I am. I look deep into eyes, holding his hand, and say, 'Baba, you look so good today.' I don't know why I say these words that have no meaning. But he smiles. The softness of his wrinkled hand has seen so many of these sunlit days. There is a strange smile that appears on his face. A knowing smile that there is someone known sitting beside him. The warm touch of a known hand is like a withered sunburnt flower that has been given life with a sprinkle of water.

A man with his full heart, who laughed loudly, is hopelessly crying in front of me. The caretaker says, 'He cries abruptly sometimes for no reason. There are days when he will be sitting for hours in the corner of the house looking outside the window and murmuring words about his daughter. There is not much left in him.' Maybe he has been waiting for me to arrive. My mother wanted this house to be converted into a woman's hostel and my grandfather abided by his only daughter whom he loved so much. Girls studying forestry and researching in fauna, are given accommodation at a minimal cost. I ask how these expenses are being met.

'Sudha sent money every month,' I am told. In the past few months, I was consuming every little scrap of new information coming my way. I knew my father used to give my mother an allowance every month for household expenses. From the time I had gone to America, there was too much to spend on. She was saving every month to send money to my grandfather after he retired. Not that he needed it, but he had this habit of donating his income to whoever was in need. Apart from this house, he'd never owned anything.

After my grandmother died, between the father and daughter, life revolved around the jungle. Nature was her friend, and the animals she visited weekly fulfilled her urge to nurture. My grandfather had refused to send my mother to a hostel, and he did not remarry. His life was his books, the forest and his loving daughter; she was his Aranyaka, the goddess of the forest. Food was not the most important thing. Knowledge was. My grandfather never expected my mother to cook for him even when she was old enough to take care of the house. I don't remember the road to the house, but I do vaguely remember Gagan, the caretaker. Grandfather's Man Friday, the life and soul of this family of two. Amma used to call him Bhaiyya and like an older brother, he protected her from the time she was a girl to becoming a woman.

My father's marriage proposal had come through my grandfather's friend. He thought my mother needed her own family. Although my father was a bit older than her, my grandmother liked his profile, an archeologist. Which meant she would travel with him and get to explore different facets of life. My mother had just finished her MSc and was waiting for her results. She was not too keen, but she did not want to make my grandfather unhappy. With the hope that she would be able to finish her PhD after marriage, she agreed to the proposal. My grandfather had assured her she would get her degree and my father added to that promise.

Life played out differently, unfortunately. Soon, it was a monochrome palette. She travelled with her new husband, not to explore different places, but to be trapped inside the four walls of home. But she would never sit still and found comfort in her books, in the plants she grew and the food she cooked. In all the little things, she found joy. After three miscarriages, my father failed to understand the problem, blaming everything on my mother. He complained about this recurring setback to my grandfather, only later to find out that it was a problem with a simple solution. My mother needed a lot of rest since her endometrium lining was weak. This time around, she took all the precautions and was on complete bedrest, which meant my father finally understood the amount of work she did to make our house a home. I was finally born, a healthy child and the 'energy' of her life.

Today, this girl sitting in front of her grandfather has lost all her energy. 'How are you Baba?' I ask, even though he doesn't look too good and probably can't even hear me. He interrupts me to say it is time for his dinner. I stand up and hug him once gain. I have no more questions for now.

A day passes exploring my grandfather's house. I meet Baba in the morning and go for a stroll around the house to see if there is anything I can remember. I have lunch, sleep for a while on the library sofa with a book in my hand. I greet the two students who have checked out to welcome two new students. I give them a faint smile which has become a habit now as they pass by the common room. The evening winter sun passes through the window, I sit calmly in the corner of the library reading one of Baba's old books on fruits of the Himalayan Range when there is a knock on the door. I open the door to a man with a bruised head. He limps his way in with confidence. He looks like someone who knows his way around the place. I welcome him keeping the door open, but he is a little startled and looks at me with a doubtful expression. I follow him to the library where he sits for a while, his strong legs shaking like a tree dancing in the wind. I wonder who he is and stand there for a while waiting for him to look at me. He marches to the sink near the kitchen, splashes water on his face, removing the mud stains and calls out in a gruff voice for the cook to make him a cup of tea. I smile awkwardly as I go to get him a towel.

I stumble on a chair and fall on my stomach. The man immediately pulls me up asking me whether I am all right. I reply in the negative and pull away from him. I notice the man looking into my eyes like I am a rare one-horned rhino. I offer him the towel; his dripping face needs it. He takes it and goes into his room, slamming the door.

This whole encounter is strange. I have to admit, he is handsome, and tall, just the kind I like. I notice his large hands. I have a fetish for men with long fingers and cabbage palms. From the corner of my eyes, I see his bruised elbow, brushed with lines; it seems like an animal had grabbed him with its fist. To me, there is more to this man than meets the eye.

⁘

It is late evening. I see him standing by the window, calming himself with a smoke. I look at him blowing the smoke in the air when he leaves the cigarette halfway as if he remembered something suddenly and walks to the vintage mahogany cupboard. I am sitting on the opposite side of a round table, looking at him opening and closing the cupboard multiple times. Finally, he closes all the open doors and sits in front of me and I feel like a woman sitting by a window, observing a story unfold. He opens a file with a hand which seems to smoke a lot and the after-effects are seen under the eyes and on the dark lips. He picks the register and flips through some bills. His words tumble out and I have to force myself to come back to the present to listen to a man I met a few hours back, 'I have been told, your grandfather has made a house agreement with his lawyer.' He goes silent again, I am about to speak but then without letting me say a word, he continues, 'I don't know much, but this decision was taken after Didi went away. I have not seen the legal papers yet.' He is quiet again. I understand that by Didi, he means my mother. Then he speaks in a voice so loud, it carries through the windows and is probably heard by the animals outside. I sit a little upright. 'We tried calling your father a couple of times, Baba at the time could speak and had asked me to send you emails but there was no reply. He also tried connecting with you Oorja, but your phone number was disconnected, and we did not have any other contact.'

He stands up; the chair screeches backwards, adding an eerie sound along with the frog croaking in the background. He looks down at me with uncertainty. Being silent all this while, curious to know more, I finally ask, 'How did you know I am Oorja?' He retorts in a standoffish manner, 'I don't need to guess. It's written all over you.' I am suddenly uncomfortable and do not understand what this stranger means.

∫

I look at him closely, his stern eyes remind me of Gagan Bhaiyya. Gagan Bhaiyya was strict but loved Amma enough to pamper her like his own daughter. He never let his sight off from my grandfather. I now see this man and it dawns on me that he is Gagan Bhaiyya's son. I don't remember his name but I vaguely remember this boy who used to come along with his father Gagan Bhaiya during the summer vacations and quietly take a place in Baba's library and read. Baba expected all of us to have books in our hands. He always said, 'You can learn every day from the smallest experiences and share your learning with every human being.' He hardly spoke then. He hardly speaks now. I have time where I can seek answers from this mysterious face who I feel possesses many secrets and also knows all about me.

'I was away, all this while. It was difficult for Baba to connect with us when we were in different corners of the world,' I raise my voice a little.

'Do not bother,' he says, sorting papers in the cardboard file.

He keeps silent and is looking at me.

'I called back,' I retort.

I never called back, says a tiny voice in my mind.

'I visited whenever I found time,' his decibel level is increasing with each sentence.

'I never visited because I was far away,' I justify myself.

'We even emailed you at your official id.'

'I left that company.' Vikrant flashes before my eyes.

I am again drawn to this angry man with unmanageable hair, wearing rugged trekking shoes and a pair of navy cargo pants.

'I am a naturalist…currently…applied for my masters… forestry management…in Australia.' He says in short, staccato sentences as he pulls out another cigarette.

'I just came back from a forest trial.'

I can see that with the bruises on your hands and there are some on your face too.

I do not say this to him. Instead I show disinterest about his whereabouts.

'Anang,' he introduces himself.

'My father…'

'Yes, I guessed it,' I cut him off mid-sentence this time.

'So, what is the way forward now, Anang?' I remember he was called Munna, but now his real name is stuck in my head. Anang, a naturalist working in the forest, is perhaps helping track some animal footprints or saving animals from poachers. Or trekking through the mountains for research work. The bruises make sense now.

'I will speak to the lawyer, now that you know…me?' he asks.

'Yes, of course,' I say.

I plonk myself on the sofa, tired of standing and in the silence of this increasingly banal conversation, I ask, 'Where is Gagan Bhaiyya?' Blowing out the last smoke in circles, Anang replies with a heavy heart, 'He had a heart attack…Baba could not handle his death.' He stammers now, 'My mother also expired a couple of months back'. I look at him, he lowers his eyes when Baba's caretaker calls,

'Anang' from the other room. There is no one around except the two of us. 'Looks like he is calling you, Anang,' I say with a smile, stressing on his name. Lost in his thoughts, leaving a cigarette he just lit, he says, 'Yes, Baba is calling me.' He refers to my grandfather as his too. He goes to meet Baba in his room, leaving me still ruminating on the sofa. There were two deaths in the family, one after the other and that has put this man suspended between his parents and our grandfather.

I am engrossed in a signature by my Baba, on a book with a date that is as old as me, when Anang comes back from my grandfather's room with only one cup of coffee for himself. 'Baba just called to check on me and ask me something and then he forgot,' he smiles, sipping his coffee, wanting to talk more. 'I have been here for a month but will need to go back now. I am worried about your grandfather and have been thinking of sending him to an old age home.' Finally, he said 'your'; but who was *he* to decide to send my grandfather to an old age home? I quickly calm myself. I was not there when my mother died. I was not there when my grandfather needed me. I cannot take care of him now. I can hardly take care of myself. I don't even know where my father is. And by the looks of it, my grandfather cannot tell me and this Anang won't be of any help either.

'The universe always conspires to provide a solution. I am glad you are here, Oorja.' Is he hinting that I will have to take my grandfather along with me? It's close to dinner time but the cook interrupts us with a kettle full of chai, and biscuits. He looks at Anang who is already drinking his coffee as if nothing has happened and walks away.

'What do you think?' He asks, now absolutely calm, while munching on a local cream biscuit which he has picked from the floral glass plate.

'As in, having biscuit for dinner? I prefer nankhatai[32] and rusk but dal-chawal[33] would be perfect now,' I reply with a smirk.

He laughs. I am surprised by the sound of his laughter.

'I have no one to look up to now,' I say.

'I have no one too.'

He seems uncomfortable revealing this to a stranger, his legs started getting fidgety again.

'I think...,' I stop, gulping my words silently, then continuing matter-of-factly, I ask him, 'Will it be a good idea to sell the house and get Baba hospitalized? I guess the expenses are soaring and there would not be enough to take care of his medical expenses.'

'Yes, this is a good idea,' this practical man replies. Is he thinking with his head or heart? We should not be sending our parents to old age homes, but this is a

---

[32]An Indian cookie
[33]Lentil and rice.

circumstance where both of us don't have a choice and we have to be practical.

I am impressed with his pragmatic point of view. I walk up to the window, stand there with my back to Anang and look at the darkness that has set in a few minutes as the sun sets, marking an end of another day with questions.

'Are you an emotional person? Or an unemotional person, Anang?'

He is not around. I am talking to an empty room.

10

The night goes by dreaming. I have strange dreams. Also, I have this habit of talking in my sleep. It's paranoia sometimes; what if your innermost secrets are no more yours? I have laughed, cried profusely and have had random conversations with unseen people. Sometimes, I can even see vivid faces. I have had conversations with my mother in my sleep. When the days are heavy, the nights become talkative. In the last job before I met Vikrant, I had a crazy argument with a colleague, which escalated to reach the boss. The argument was about an American woman who had a bee farm. I got to know about her through a researcher who had told me about the 'Bee Maker'.

I was supposed to run this documentary about the bee maker but there was another woman working in the same group, who saw this as an opportunity and pestered the boss till she gave it to her. As soon as I found out, I flew into a rage, barged into the boss's office and gave her a piece of my mind. I did not wait for her to say sorry. I practically flew out of her office even as her face turned red with bitterness. She was fuming while I was swelling with pride knowing I did the right thing.

I called the researcher home that night. All the while we had sex, I was rough with him, slapping him hard, trying to shake off my office frustration. He did not mind it at all; for someone who does not like anyone sharing the bed with her, I made an exception and asked him to stay back after seeing his tired slapped face. After all, he was too lazy after the aggressive sex to go to his house. In the quietness of a cold winter night, we snuggled under my blanket. Except the fridge kept making strange sounds, punctuating our cozy night in.

After a while, in his deep sleep, his snore kept gaining a higher and higher octave. I started talking in my sleep, screaming gibberish Hindi, with my pitch higher than his, like a newsroom debate. I was trashing the boss, the honey story stealer. The timid-looking researcher was my victim that night. I kicked him in my sleep, slapped him again and again.

Next morning, with no recollection of the previous night, I saw an empty side of the bed. He had left. Obviously, who wants to be beaten up by sleep talker who can get really angry? I sat on the bed like a zombie looking at the scattered kitchen table. The researcher had given me a slap on my face. He never came back, but I went back to the job the next morning as if nothing had happened and my boss behaved as if nothing had happened. All of us met the Bee Maker. After all, the bees believe in unity.

※

There is a knock on the door. It is 5:30 AM. My groggy eyes open to Mr Big Hands, looking frail but high on energy. 'Why did you wake me up?' I mutter, half asleep. He laughs looking at me. He is more relaxed than yesterday. 'I wanted to check whether you would want to come with me…for the safari. I am going along with…,' he is choosing his words carefully, haltingly, '…a European documentary film maker Rafael and his videographer. I thought you might be interested.' This man is standing on the opposite side of the spectrum. Yesterday he was grey, today he looks like colours are mixed with the grey. My eyes shine. 'So kind of you to think about me. Isn't it too early to ask me out?' I joke. His eyes are doing all the talking. I become a little conscious that I am not wearing anything under my T-shirt. I am briefly tempted to accept the safari offer but refuse because I really want to get some sleep.

I decline and he whispers a good night and turns his back to me as I stand there; my door is still open. I see him coming back, my heartbeat increasing with every footstep he takes. He limps really close to me; I can feel his breath. I look at him as he shoos away a baby lizard which is just above my hand. I jump backwards with a jerk. He is not looking at me; he is looking at the lizard making its way up. I wish I had jumped towards him. He is in a hurry as his phone emits light through his pocket, illuminating the dark alley like a disco room. He has a 'birds chirping' ringtone ringing continuously. His 'He... llo' merges with my 'bye' as the sun rises, and I go off to sleep once again.

∫

I sleep really well until afternoon, after the early morning meeting with Anang. I take a nice warm bath and get into my jeans and embroidered kurta to have lunch. I am hoping that I would meet Anang but he is not around. The two girls I saw yesterday are there too. I overhear them discussing their thesis. Everyone in this world is trying to achieve something. These two girls are trying to make their future. Like them, there are many who would be appearing for exams, attending classes, submitting their work. Whereas I do not have any achievement yet. I quietly eat my dal rice with a spoon of curd in it, just like the way Amma relished hers. My head is bent, and I am looking at every morsel on my plate. When you have all the time in the world, you start looking at the smaller things more closely.

I ask the cook for more rice and then ask whether my grandfather has eaten. The cook tells me that Baba is sleeping; like most days, his time passes by sleeping. He also insists that I meet him after he wakes up before he goes back to sleep again. I nod, taking the rice from him, adding more dal and a pinch of curd. I am eating silently when I hear, 'Is there anything left to eat?' I look up to see Mr Big Hands. 'I was speaking to Baba about you,' he says. 'How thoughtful, but wasn't Baba sleeping?' 'Yes, but he can hear with his eyes closed,' he replies, somewhat cheekily. 'What did you tell him…about me?' I can feel my cheeks turn to electrifying pink. He does not answer. I do not bother to ask how his morning was. Nor do I overtly react to his cold and hot attitude. I quietly continue eating, hoping he would grab a chair and sit next to me.

From New York to a remote forest exploring a spiritual, unknown side, life has indeed taken an acute turn. He sits in front of me. I blush even more. He looks fazed and is perspiring like he just finished a boxing match. I want to ask him if everything is okay. He gets up to splash some water on his face. I sense he has a lot to tell me and I want to hear it all. He is quiet again with marks on his forehead that have dried up to show erratic lines.

The house. Grandfather. My father. I am in no hurry to finish all the crisscrossing conversations, so I remain silent. He is absorbed in his food, gulping down mouthfuls with his left hand. The girls have left, and the cook has melted into the background. It is only the two of us. In the sharp silence, there is a sudden sound of wailing from afar. The voices become clearer as they come near. It is the cook and the caretaker with shocked expressions as they come towards us.

Our grandfather is no more, we are told in between sobs. Anang was the last one to see him and, in fact, the last words my grandfather heard may have been about me. Anang and I rush to my grandfather's room to see a quiet peaceful face. He looks beautiful. I do not have tears but Anang sobs audibly. I suddenly feel alone. But Anang's loss in this moment seems somehow bigger than mine. 'I was wrong, I should have not even had thoughts of leaving him in his old age.' He keeps repeating, 'I was wrong,' crying profusely. 'Maybe he guessed it. This was his way to leave us without giving anyone trouble,' he sobs.

Anang is inconsolable. This time he is standing at the other edge of the spectrum. Death brings sobering thoughts and heavy emotions together. Our Baba has left everything as is. Lying on his bed in peace, he is telling us that nothing is more important than being alive now with the little joys we have.

I keep looking at Baba. 'He looks so bright,' I say without holding back my tears anymore. I start sobbing, not so much for him as for myself, at my own situation.

At the end of the day, humans are fragile; they may

act tough in front of the world but there is only so much acting one can do.

Holding my grandfather's cold hands is comforting even after he is gone, and I only wish I had gotten to spend a little more time with him. I wish I had spent a little more time with my mother too. The afternoon turns into evening, even as time stands still. There is an eerie silence with the sound of people who have come to visit him, as he is laid at the entrance of the house below the Sal trees. The shadows of the trees make the night look even darker; as if there is no beginning and no end. Life is complicated but death is simple. Baba did not want anything elaborate, I am told. He did not want a procession or rituals, none of the phoniness that comes with the end. Some people start leaving after paying their condolences, the closest ones follow Anang who is leading, carrying his broken emotions which seem even heavier to bear. When you see death from such close quarters, fear goes away. One day, each one of us will go. A feeling of impermanence settles in me as I stand there, lighting everything in a new perspective.

Living and dying.
All the same.
You are born to live.
You live to die.
No one can escape.

The truth lies in what you see.
Here we are.
One on earth.
Other in the sky.

11

Everyone has gone to the crematorium except me. I cannot bear to go. My tired swollen eyes are sleepy in the wee hours of the morning, in the library of an empty house of sadness. In my sleep, my mind takes me back to the time I was staying in a PG while doing my under-graduation in the university. I shared a room with an Indian girl, her presence promising to provide the familiar comfort of shared food and language. Trisha was from the southern part of India and belonged to an engineering family. Both her parents were techies and she was studying analytics; her dream was to get into an Ivy League school and feature in the under-30 power list one day. I had no such ambition.

We were different and yet being in a foreign land had fortuitously brought us together. I had hoped I would get inspired by her drive, but no such inspiration beckoned. The roomie ended up creating a weird environment with her obsessive behaviour that ranged from an attachment to her space, her things, her food and her love for horror movies. Every night, she played one such film on her television with volume so loud, I felt it would deafen me as I snuggled deeper in my bed, in the little space I could find that wasn't encroached upon by her. She was not bothered about what I felt in the least.

Accepting people who behave and act in a certain way that was in no way okay had become a part of me. The real horror in my life continued for a long time. I never realized when it started affecting me and I finally found the courage to ask for a change of roommate.

∫

I scream at an unknown figure; I feel like the house is haunted and I am stuck inside. There is no human around except the skeleton of my grandfather. The smoke around his body feels like a cloud of little shapeless skulls hovering towards me. I scream once again trying to defend myself. My legs are kicking something as if I am trying to free myself from the clutches of his skeleton hands. I am shaking and then I hear a thud. I am crying and I feel like I am being dragged into a black hole. I feel a cold touch on my face. My eyes open on the couch. Anang's tired but concerned face is hovering above me. I am suddenly awake and sweating. I look at him, confused at my own condition.

'You were screaming, Oorja. What happened?' His groggy eyes are concerned.

His hands are on my shoulders. The sun is still not up. The pale yellowish grey light falls on his face and in the shadow, I can only see his eyes shining. I cannot move. His hands shake me again, this time more firmly. I have turned into a rock, unmovable and silent. He moves me closer to him and slowly puts my head on his chest. His heartbeat feels calm and reassuring. I close my eyes again; my face is feeling his warmth through his comforting hands.

Anang is my winged man. I keep looking at him and close my eyes seeing him vanish away, going back to deep sleep to be woken up again, 'Get up Oorja. Is this the time to sleep? Who sleeps so late when there has been a death in the house?' A woman's voice is scolding me as I open my eyes with great effort to a strange face staring at me. She leaves me continuing her 'Oorja' chants.

I get up without any choice and walk across the house to see a storm of humans in every corner of the house. Each of them looks at me with empathy. I can hear snatches of their conversation. 'Poor girl, she is all alone now. Even the last one of the family is absconding.' 'Look, she is here after all this while. Where was she when her family really needed her?' Even as I hear buzzing voices all around me, my eyes are searching through the crowd for the one person who is not in sight. I go back to my room and close the door behind me. I have a splitting headache which should recede with some sleep. Everyone, even the ones not closely associated to Baba, has a say on what needs to be done. Where is Anang? I wonder.

Then, as I am about to sleep, as if sensing my thoughts, the caretaker comes to tell me that Anang has asked me to visit the Local municipal office as soon as I can. I decide to go immediately without blinking an eye. The road to the government office dealing with building and mortage was not very far; the caretaker was kind enough to drop me as it was on his way to the central market square.

He shows me the entrance, I hear voices of people from a distance as I enter a room full of commotion. In a small town, everyone has some legal issue which looks like the lines on maps. Brothers divided in blue and red lines. The land their father owned divided in brown and grey lines. The brothers born from one mother fight over money. An ego that raises its head and says, 'I don't care about our relationship anymore.'

I see Anang sitting on a wooden bench in the corner of a pale yellowish worn-down building, awaiting his turn. Legs trembling again like he has been hit by a thunderstorm, temples perspiring, he is watching the documentary of the most powerful tigress, who played a very important role in regenerating the tiger population across the forest region. He is so engrossed that he doesn't notice me sit quietly next to him, observing his deep interest for the enchanting forests.

Coming from a workplace where we would observe the

interplay of culture and the dynamics of human relationship with spaces, I am noticing the various facets of law and the nature of human conduct in the face of it. I absorb my surroundings, noticing the middle-aged woman crying quietly in the corner even as her son is screaming at her. The brothers who are arguing with a legal paper in hand as a timid lawyer waits impatiently, looking at his watch. Anang has a cardboard card with 12 written on it. He seems to be in a pensive mood and still does not notice I am sitting beside him.

I open my floral cloth bag to get the book I picked up from Baba's library. What will happen to all his books? I wonder. Could I carry them with me as his legacy? Each book has something to offer. Of fact, fiction, ideas, stories, seeking truth in the questions I am asking. A magical world. A bibliomancy. There is so much more to books than adorning a bookshelf which is hardly dusted.

Anang stifles a yawn and stretches his shoulders, finally noticing the stranger beside him. I pretend to ignore him. He taps on the book I am reading, '*A Cloud in the Sky?*'

I nod.

'When did you come?'

'Long before you noticed.'

'Did you get your identity card?' he asks, in a brisk, no-nonsense manner.

'Yes. But why did you ask the caretaker to call me here?' I ask.

He looks strangely wistful; I furrow my brows and wonder as he scrutinizes my identity card. He slowly tells me that Baba transferred the house in his name. He did not know until last evening, when the lawyer came with the papers. He did not understand whether there was a confusion or whether it was a mistake. He read it through to see his name printed on the pale-yellow paper signed by Baba's old hands.

He had never bothered to check. Why would he?

I never bothered to ask. Why would I?

The little speaker fixed on the old walls calls out a series of number. On hearing number twelve, Anang stands up with relief after the long wait. He walks towards a government official who has twelve written on a cardboard placed on the table. I follow him, uninvited, catching up with him. Looking at the atmosphere around and seeing Baba's lawyer who was already there attending to other clients, Anang says to me, 'Don't know what I am going to do with this big house.' The lawyer waved his hand at us from afar.

'I can still transfer the house in your name. After all, you are his own flesh and blood. That's why I asked you to come here.' The lawyer who looks as old as my father calls out for Anang. He is impatient now, assuming there is some confusion, 'I hope there is no disparity? You are Oorja Chaturvedi Madam? The owner's granddaughter?' I look at him and say, 'Yes'.

Through his steel-rimmed glasses, he browses through the paper for validity. I sit beside him in awe. There is always a first time for everything you do, which allows you to grow. In my life, the map of my borders of evolution are growing. Today, they have expanded by leaps of gratitude.

'I may be his blood on a legal paper, but you are his blood in every way that matters,' I tell him with a light heart.

Assured, he nervously signs each leaf of the legal document that makes him the owner of the house my mother grew up in. The diaries with scribbled notes she left behind. The touch her father left behind. The trees that grew with them. That protected them in all seasons. The cracked walls that tells a story of passing time, of the many who have had a relationship with it, even after they are gone. This home, along with all the emotions felt in it, belongs to him.

Anang signs his initials on each page. As the lawyer checks the pages closely, Anang looks impatient now. When the lawyer turns to the last page, Anand stands up flexing his fingers. The lawyer looks at him with irritation, showing him the empty spaces that had not been filled, 'Please write your postal address here with your mobile number and date.' Anang, who is ready to leave, asks restlessly, 'Is it really necessary to write the current address? It's already there in the agreement.' He relentlessly refuses to write the address. The elderly lawyer does not budge, 'What is important is important.' Anang is forced to put down the address, his restless feet are tapping like a flamingo's. I intervene by touching his shoulders to give him comfort. He retracts as if I am an evil energy sitting by his side, making him do things he does not like. Of course, it's important to put the address, phone number and email id on the property papers. I remember doing that even when I was discharged from hospital. He sloppily starts writing, stopping to think hard before putting down a number. This must be the longest anyone has taken to write down their number, I think. The documentation is testing my patience. The lawyer is now smiling through his paan-stained teeth, he shakes Anang's hand and hugs him like a long-lost son. He is the sole owner of my grandfather's colonial estate. Anang leaves without acknowledging gratitude towards the lawyer.

'Does this make us brother and sister?' I blush and ask, running behind him without any self-respect. 'No,' he is back to his no-nonsense tone as he marches ahead like a warrior without looking back. I run back to retrieve Anang's house papers.

12

A day goes by, there is a certain, unexplained tension between us. I want to talk to him about my father but refrain from doing so. The next day, on a sultry afternoon, we are removing books, one by one, from the shelves and putting them in cartons. I am slower than him, reading through the covers I find interesting. He, on the other hand, is at it with military efficiency.

'What are we going to do about these?' he suddenly asks, my ears perking up at the 'we'.

'I don't know,' I say. He was exceptionally quiet yesterday and the day before and I can sense an indifference or is it just the way he is, a man of few words? I do not pursue the conversation and the books keep being displaced from where they belong—the bookshelf. Once shut, they are rarely opened till someone senses their need on a lonely day. On a ruminating day. On a documenting day. On a day when we seek company. On a day when we are waiting for someone. Until then, they are just there, waiting in the bookshelf, quiet and still.

The cook is singing along with the radio which is playing an old classic. Anang seems like he is trying to decide what to say and I am looking at him quietly. Longingly waiting for a reaction. But he is so engrossed that his silence seems to be forbidding anyone against disturbing him. By the time we finish piling the boxes with books in complete silence, it is evening. The room has no space to walk. The sofa and table are pushed to the corners. The boxes take center stage. With dust all over us, I follow him as he goes into his room which is opposite to mine and shuts the door on me.

Back in my bathroom, I stand on white tiles as the water pours on me from head to toe. A mirage explodes as the drops of waters trickle down. Slowly. Some stay. Some burst. Some just slide through the edges of my fingers and toes. In a fraction of a second, they are gone. The warm water flowing over me gives me a little relief. My body is still fatigued from the lack of sound sleep. The warm bath did good to my senses, but I am groggy and hungry. I open my door, Anang's room is still closed. I want to knock but walk to the dining area which is empty. The only sounds I can hear is my stomach grumbling. Freshly made evening snacks have been placed in steel bowls. I gobble a plate of pakoras with ketchup and then feel like my stomach might explode. I feel bloated and need a walk. Walking down the back door which opens up to the vast forest garden of the estate, I feel a sense of ownership for a place which, although attached to my lineage, is not mine anymore. I see a shadow sitting far on a wooden bench surrounded by foliage, deep in the forest garden.

He is in a meditative pose looking up at the starry night beside a giant Cannonball tree that has flowers spreading to the trunk. The pink and red flowers with a tinge of yellow are sprinkled on the green grass as the tree shines brightly with the light of the moon. Anang picks up the fallen flowers near him and looks at them lovingly as I go and sit next to him once again, not disturbing his silence. Both of us look at the moon.

Every day is a different version of itself.
It tells stories, each a different one.
Of life in motion.
Of life in stillness.
Of a lantern on a dark night.
Of solitude and silver linings.
Of the circle of new beginnings.
Of stale ends.
Of a circle of gratitude called you.
Called me.
Called the moon.

Hearing him say these poetic lines feels surreal, as if this night cannot get any better. Each word is spoken slowly. Sometimes strong. Sometimes just right. There is a silence mixed with the strong fragrance of the flowers that is spreading around us with his engrossed thoughts and deeply felt presence.

'You know Oorja...'

I look into his eyes; every letter of his sporadic words matters to me.

'Baba had sowed the seeds of this mystical tree when your mother was very young.' I feel as if I can see Amma in the light passing through the intertwined branches of the tree. 'There must have been so many nights when my mother must have sat here and mapped the trail of her life as she saw it unfold.' Anang leans towards me, making himself comfortable and asks, 'What would it be like to sit with our loved ones and hear them speak on such a blooming night?' His eyes light up in the glow of the white light. 'Do you know what it will be like?' I ask myself truthfully. Then I ask him in a low tone, 'Do you know every star reflects a human? What's your star?' I ask. Anang cannot gauge what I mean by this statement. He raises his thick eyebrows in a quizzical manner. We do not take the conversation forward. He looks mysterious to me, sometimes loving, sometimes boorish, altogether moody. I hesitantly hear, '21 July,' as if he is trying to remember his own star sign. His contradictory emotions and behaviour is just like my mother. His birthday falls two days after Amma's.

Picking a fallen beauty, I sniff this multi-layered secretive cannonball flower while waiting for him to speak. The strong fragrance almost intoxicates me while he is still looking up at the moon. I maintain the silence and he continues to look at the moon and then towards me.

'I always waited to see this tree after the rains, so full of leaves. It is a symbol of love which will never shrink even after everyone is gone. Baba wanted me to be like Shiva's tree, emitting Naga Linga flowers every day, lighting up the whole universe.'

This time I look at the tree closely. It is towering over us and oozes so much strength and energy.

'Why are you crying?' I ask, seeing tears rolling down his face.

'You won't understand, Oorja. Because if you did, you wouldn't be so lost all this while; you are damn selfish. What kind of a child were you to a mother who craved her child's presence? You were never there. You were not there even when she was gone,' he finally says.

'Do you even understand what you said right now?' I stand up to walk towards the boundary. Anger has taken hold of me. It has been a long time since rage has consumed me with such intensity. He follows behind me; I can hear his footsteps crushing the dry leaves. I walk faster. I start running. The leaves in the dark woods are making crunching noises and, in the darkness surrounding me, I can see Amma's house emitting light. As I run, even a few steps feel like a huge distance, I pause and hold myself against a Sal tree, panting hard with the cold breeze blowing. Leaves fall around me; I look up for the first time focusing on the moon shining through the dark tangle of trees. I have never felt as inundated with emotion as tonight.

'Sorry,' I hear him say. I can feel that he means what he says.

I move close to him, my eyes staring at his lips. He freezes for a moment, not knowing whether to let go. 'I am lost,' I whisper as my lips touch his. The taste of the lingering woody essence on his lips is divine. The kiss itself is soft and supple. Our lips intertwine like ivy creepers. Not letting go as if he has been waiting for this for a long time. Slow. Then fast. Then slow, matching the rhythm of the trees in the wind. We are swaying to an unknown melody. The moon is still shining, acting as a spotlight on us. My blushing eyes gleam with unspoken words.

Everything said was forgotten. We walk back to the house, hand in hand, slowly with only the soft sound of leaves as we step on them. As we see the little light from the boundary, his hands move away from mine. I do not understand why. I can see the guard frantically looking for us. He shines his torchlight and it hits our eyes. 'It's dark out there and anything can happen,' he fearfully says. I smile in my mind. Anang is impassive. We have a secret between us. My happy moment is interrupted again by the guard murmuring to himself, 'Thank God, you are safe,' as he guides us with this torchlight inside the boundary of Anang's estate.

'Will you have a cup of tea too?' Anang finally says, as he asks one for himself. 'I don't want to mess with my current taste,' I laugh, crossing boundaries. He does not react. 'I need to ask you a few important things before we call it a night.' Settling himself on the cane chair, he takes his phone out from one of the pockets of his khaki shorts. I am still standing in front of him looking at his thick hair, 'Can we do this tomorrow?' I ask, longing to feel his touch again. 'No, it will be a little late,' he says, still engrossed in his phone, restlessly typing a message.

I try but cannot see what he is writing clearly. Our old friend 'silence' has joined us again. His keypad is still clicking; I close my eyes playing back the moment we just had under the moonlight. It is a beautiful feeling to see the whole thing in colour again and again, until I am interrupted by a voice, 'Your chai is here.'

I have no option but to slurp my tea as he finishes his frantic messaging. He is trying to determine how to articulate what he wants to tell me. I can see it in his eyes.

Still sipping the tea, and looking at the white floral English teacup, he rearranges himself and leans back, making himself even more comfortable. 'I will be leaving tomorrow…for Delhi…you can stay here for as long as you like. Also, this is your home.' I interrupt him, 'No this is...not my house. This is yours. Rightfully so.' For the first time, I feel like I am making sense. I am ready for a more mature conversation. 'I have been feeling that you are not comfortable that this estate has been given to me,' he says hesitatingly. He continues, 'Before I leave, this doubt has to be cleared from my mind. I would have not felt anything if we had not met. But destiny has got us here and it's very important for me to know that you are absolutely sure about this. Because if you feel that this belongs to you, then I'll give it to you and have nothing to do with it.' He finishes his tea and asks for more.

I had the sudden urge to ask him why he did not transfer the house to me if he feels so guilty. But before I can say anything, he offers to transfer the house in my name. I convince him not to do so and eventually the discussion ends. I change the subject and ask, 'What are you going to do with this estate? I feel you should make a boutique nature house and have people from all over the world come to stay.' He is quiet and says in a sad tone, 'I won't be here to see the world come. I will be gone in two months. We will have to close this house for a while or, if you agree, I can sell it. We can divide the money; it will be of use to you.'

I don't want to do it. This is my childhood. My memory. My life.

Both of us echo the same sentiment but say something else.

Sudha Guest House will continue, we both decide. Our lives too will continue down their own paths. 'But I don't have your number,' I say, suddenly realizing this after we exchange promises to keep in touch.

He begins that nervous tick of his: absentmindedly tapping his feet.

His fingers run on me like a glow of light rising, making its way to evoke a sense of yearning. He pulls me closer and whispers, 'When we need to connect, the universe will find a way.'

'What is this moment?' I ask.

'The…beginning,' he says cryptically and gets up to leave.

I sit there holding on to the scent of his warmth.

Is it the beginning?

Or the beginning of an end?

⌁

The morning light has a different story to tell than yesterday. Anang is getting ready to leave, with his rucksack on his back and an olive laptop bag in his hand. The Jeep is now revving impatiently when he asks the driver to shut down the four-wheeler. He walks towards me and I stand there, feeling strangely low. I will be alone all over again. He stands in front of me and looks around to see if anyone is noticing us. His face comes closer. This is the moment I have been waiting for. There is no one around.

'See you sometime,' he says awkwardly.

'Come with me to the mountains...,' I whisper, holding his hand tightly.

Silence.

'Please don't do this to me. I am on an unknown road,' I say again.

'The river shines reflecting the rays of the sun and you will find your reflection there in the mountains,' he replies. How poetic! I gather my courage to resolve this situation and move closer to him, murmuring softly, 'I will scream loudly if you go now.' The love and pain I am feeling tumble out through a war of words. 'Scream! As loudly as you want. Let your voice out, it's been long, right? Scream, let the Gods hear your pain, for taking away your mother from you,' he says, somewhat angrily. His breathing is laboured and he leaves me with his unaffectionate eyes as a parting gift.

He leaves and doesn't turn back, without even a 'Call me' or 'Let's meet when you are in Delhi'. He leaves me speechless. How can I cry for you, my dear one? Yesterday was just an 'after-dark' moment which disappeared into thin air, leaving complex emotions mixed with anger and love. What happened yesterday has been forgotten today. The trees are swaying with the force of an angry wind. The grey clouds are changing their destination. Not a single bird in the sky. Tears are rolling down my face and my heart is throbbing with anguish.

From where your divine love flows
Like the first ray of sun.
Shining on the white, gleaming mountains.
Reflecting your light
I will see you there.
My dear one.

I read my father's haphazard words once again. The words that I could not comprehend before, present themselves clearly now. A random address written vertically on the note by my father with a slanting hand seems to speak to me, 'Anang is gone. I must leave too.'

13

All of us look like an overflowing box of toffies in a child's hand. The taxi driver wants to fill up the seats of his last ride of the day so that he can take a few days off to be with his wife. They are expecting a child any day and he wants to rush home. I am curious and cannot resist asking him how long he has been married; he looks too young to have a child. 'Ten months,' he sheepishly answers. I am sitting beside him and next to me is a little girl whose mother is sitting behind with what seems like a newborn baby, perhaps a few months old. She must be going back to her husband. Beside her is a man who looks like her husband, who pays no attention to the child, even as the mother is hassled and tries to calm her howling child as we climb up the mountain. There is also a middle-aged man, who seems to be a fruit-selling businessman. He finds an opportunity for business looking at me, perhaps hoping I will be his future customer. He tells me everything about his farm in the hills. How he grows organic fruit that is sent across to the super stores in metros. I nod from time to time, not having the option to jump out of the car. Just then the woman with the baby throws up. The car stops by a corner. I need some air. The address on my father's note is as good as not being written. This is his way to trouble me and make me find him so that he can say, 'See Oorja, I told you, when you try hard, you can accomplish anything you want. Nothing comes easy, you see.' I have always had this secret desire to travel with him on a motorbike on the wide roads of Ladakh, where there are mountains of different shades all around as far as the eye can see. I want to learn swimming in an open blue lake. I think of an image of a father's hand holding his little girl afloat. When will I find him?

The valley has a beautiful river flowing through it. I keep staring at it for a long time trying to remember something which has been bothering me from the time I woke up in the wee hours of this morning. The feeling that I have lost someone I had only just got to know is still sinking in. The river is flowing calmly, splashing against the unmoving shore. In my dream last night, a boat was moving. I am scared of water but in my dream, I was rowing a small boat in a wide ocean. In the vastness, a tiny me was alive. There is a relevance of the dream to my current situation. The story from my subconscious mind that bothers me.

The dream of being in a boat has not left my mind. Everything happens for a reason and this is another one. The wide sky with floating clouds is giving me signs about the next steps I have to take. In ancient times, the boat is considered an important symbol of survival. There is a belief that the souls of the dead cross a river and wither away. My mother must be crossing the ocean along with me. She is guiding me to the exact location of my father and also indicating my progress spiritually. There is a hole in the boat. The sea is restless. I must still have a strong desire to survive. Besides, these are obstacles that I needed, to start a new life.

The rest of the drive is calm, with the businessman talking incessantly, and the child crying intermittently when she is hungry. The little girl sitting next to me is looking outside the window enjoying the wind on her face. I wonder what she is thinking. I wonder what the man who bore this child is thinking. I turn around to look at him. His eyes are closed. I look at his wife. The baby is sucking milk from her breasts.

Every time I see a pregnant lady, I imagine a graphic image in technicolour, straight out of an erotic pulp fiction where a man and woman are together. I cannot help but wonder about the night when the conception happened. I even weave a story from my imagination. How did they touch each other? Were they tender? What was that moment like? Was it a dull afternoon or a night full of promise?

Was it discussed, or did it just happen naturally? Did they really want a child? Was she happy? Was he happy? These are some of the questions that are evoked by their tired faces. Tired after that night. Happy through the nine months. Happy about the baby.

My daydreaming is interrupted by a loud bang and the driver honking continuously. My eyes turn to the kid who has banged her head on the dashboard. She is crying loudly. The vehicles behind us is making a ruckus honking. It seems like the whole mountain range is screaming on the top of its voice, asking for help. The mother with the child is safe. The baby is howling, this time in her father's arms. Thank God, everyone seems to be alive. I pick the girl and stand outside screaming at the driver. I do not understand what just happened. The small car in front of us hit a bike that had been racing in the opposite direction. Our driver driving behind could not control his speed and banged the car.

I am extremely agitated and refuse to sit in the bus. The driver apologizes profusely, 'My wife is waiting, and I need to reach.' 'Then why the hell were you driving like a maniac? Your wife would have lost you forever!' I accuse him in a fit of rage. I am on the verge of slapping him but the little girl's mother calms me down. 'I don't want to go,' I scream. The sounds of the horns are increasing behind us but that does not stop me from screaming at a sleep-deprived human who is driving overtime to earn a little extra so that he can spend time with his pregnant wife. A long line of vehicles, like a line of ants, is waiting because of me. As I look at the mountain range, my heart melts. It is filled with humans in each of the vehicles, big and small, all eager to reach their destination, accomplish their tasks. Go back. Come back. Or simply travel around.

My mother lost her life in a split second. When the most important person of our lives goes away because of someone else's mistake, the lives of many others also get affected immeasurably. Human error cannot be rectified. Lives cannot come back. How do you know that when you step out today, you will necessarily return?

The driver is as slow as a turtle now. The businessman sits in the front keeping the sleepy driver engaged. The little girl on my lap has slept off with her head on my shoulder. She seems to find comfort in the rhythm of my heartbeat that has slowed down seeing her peacefully sleeping. I look through the hazy window as the mountains, etched with numerous stories of travellers, pass me by.

Reflect.
You. Me
All in transit.
Half. Full.
A fragile
Life.

PART 3

14

The phone is ringing continuously but there is no answer from the other side, I double-check the number written by me on my father's crumpled notes. The number is correct. Why is Anang not picking up the phone? I got his number by chance, not because he wanted to give it to me. That afternoon when I was sitting with Anang at the lawyer's office, I had quickly noted it down in my mind. But then the file he forgot gave me an opportunity to copy the number on a piece of torn paper with a pen I had grabbed from the lawyer.

Anang is unreachable and untraceable, like my father. I return the mobile phone to the businessman who is busy chatting with a middle-aged man at the tea stall at the Bhimtal market square where we were dropped by the taxi. I am waiting for him to finish his tea so that he can drive me in his own car further up to my father's house.

The two people are talking about the growing rate of road accidents. I put my head down pretending not to listen, especially after what happened today. An hour's journey through the winding mountain road has turned to three.

We drive from the market uphill to the lazy residential lane. Looking at my impatient face, he assures me the house is not too far away now. The businessman I hitched a ride with lives two roads ahead, facing the beautiful mountains. He read the address a couple of times and immediately knew where it was. We are on the road and reach my destination soon after. We finally stand outside a rusted gate which feels as if no one has given it love for a long time. Unprepared for the change in the weather here, I am shivering from a lack of adequate clothes. Without answering his obvious questions, I jump over the gate and follow the huge wild bushes that are growing along the slanting path down to a beautiful house. It does not look very old. The path takes us to a locked house. The bell is not working. I can feel it in the unwelcoming atmosphere, that my father was never here. I walk around the house to see a desolate vast patch of land that is stretching as far as my eyes can go. I walk further down the hilly patch and stand at the end of the valley, looking back at a house on the top, imagining fruits blossoming in front of us. Everything in this world looks so beautiful. It is difficult to leave this place and it feels as if it was made for me. *I will come back.* Not knowing whether I will be true to my words, I leave a lifeless house on a hill to take care of itself and return to the waiting car, disappointed.

I wonder where my father has gone. The car is driving fast on a narrow lane; I ask the businessman, whose name is Vinod Rawat, to slow down. He says to me, 'Everyone in the mountain is in a hurry although everything around them is slow. They know that they have to make things happen before the sun sets. They know there is only one way to go up and the same way goes down. There is no time to waste. People walk for miles in the hills and are never tired. With the first rays of the morning sun, the day starts. With the sun setting, the day ends. That's mountain life.'

'But life can come to an end if you drive recklessly,' I furiously point out, all the while thinking of my mother. 'Take me to the nearest police station,' I demand. He sheepishly smiles as he drives me to the main police station. I ask Vinod if he knew anyone in this house we just visited. He tells me that he does not live here. He continues, 'I live here but I don't live here. This is my hometown. I have business here. Delhi is where my family is. I come here once every fifteen days to check on the orchard.' It all makes sense now, I silently comfort myself.

'How many questions will you ask me?' the cop we meet at the police station asks me. I need only one answer, 'Do you know anyone by the name of Mr Vishal Chaturvedi?' I ask him for the third time. He looks at the papers in his file and then at the address on the piece of paper handwritten by my father. The cop takes off his spectacles and rubs his eyes. I am still waiting for an answer. I ask Vinod to leave. He insists he wants to stay. He looks harmless and I let him be a spectator in this conversation between the cop and me. He will also give me a ride back to the town. I stand there in silence as the middle-aged cop keeps reading the address. I give him time. Finally, he looks up at me and asks in a low tone, 'Can you give me his phone number?' The cop is testing my patience and I answer back sarcastically, 'You think I have not tried calling him? His phone is switched off!'

I am starting to get agitated and before I conclude that coming to the police station is a fruitless exercise, he asks me to recount the series of events that made me visit his police station. He also wants to know the relatives of my father's where he stayed in Lucknow and also the people he must have met before writing this note. 'How am I supposed to know?' I ask. He nods his acquiescence. But then he adds that he won't be able to help me if I cannot help him. Vinod intervenes after his eyes flit between the two of us, as if he is watching us play a tennis match of question and answer. He requests the cop to hear me out and be a little patient with me. He even addresses me as 'Bichari Bachhi.[34]' I sit down on the chair and finally write

---

[34] Poor girl

down what the cops asks me.

'Who are the people who stay next to your house?'

'Srivastav Aunty and her husband, Mr Srivastav.'

'Who are the people who your father must have met?' (As written in one of the pages in the diary.)

'The professor at the university.

Verma uncle's travel shop.

Rajan Uncle's stationery shop.'

'Any uncles or aunts?'

'No, my father was an only child. And so was my mother and so am I.'

'Anywhere in particular he might go or any particular person he might meet?' I note down the places I can think of half-heartedly in the register.

Benaras. 'Don't know why, maybe in memory of my mother, Mrs Sudha Chaturvedi.'

The policeman looks at me doubtfully. And marks it with a question mark.

Corbett. He did not go. I went. I do not mention it here.

Jungle Guest House. My grandfather's home. I don't think he is there, otherwise I would have known. The staff would have told me. Anang would have told me. So, this place is also useless for the police register.

Anang. Why would he want to know about Anang? He is my secret.

'This is it,' I say firmly.

I put the register down and look at him like a good child who has just finished her assignment. He goes through the single sheet and asks me to sign it along with the date. He wants my contact number. I ask him if my email address would do. 'Messaging is faster for us, just call and speak,' he replies. I look at Vinod for approval. He is eager to give his number. But how would giving his number help me? I write down Anang's number instead. Which, I knew by heart now.

The cop asks me to go back to Lucknow. 'I will call you'. The cop does not mean what he says. I give up and do not depend on that phone call. I don't even know why I came to the police. What would I do even if I find my father? What am I going to say to him? Taking Vinod's phone, I dial Anang's number on a whim, knowing deep in my heart that I will be with him soon. I decide to go to Delhi to meet him.

Vinod drives me to Nainital and drops me at a hotel which he had already booked for me while we were driving back. After which he will drive back to the hills. I thank him for his help. An unknown person has become a friend. His nonstop chatter helped me unlock one part of this mystery. As he drops me, Vinod asks me to connect with him in Delhi when he is back home. I have taken down the details of his place in case I need to go and stay in his house with his wife. By now, even she knows my story, thanks to the many video calls she made to her husband.

I wave this Samaritan goodbye one last time, not knowing if I will meet him again.

The room is beautiful. At night, the mountains are as dark as my mind. The morning view will hopefully soften my distress. Under the shower, my tired self wants more than the warmth of the water dripping through my feet, which have walked miles. His lips on mine. His big hands holding me tight. I can feel his touch. Him holding me tight, warming me on a cold night like today. The mind being out of control is good sometimes. It wanders wherever it wants to. Sometimes to the mountains. Sometimes to the sky. Tonight, it takes me far away on a cloud carrying me to another land of wildflowers that grow to make a bed of love. Tonight is like no other night. Because he is on my mind. The droplets of water evaporate with each passing thought. 'Take me with you,' in my mind, I had pleaded with him again and again. My body trembles with hunger.

15

The travel is monotonous this time around, as I have nothing to think of, apart from my father. The outside looks the same. I decide to stop reliving my memories. But the situation requires me to unfold some memories. My lost father remains untraceable; with this dejection, I am still trying to find positivity by living in the moment, looking forward to meet Anang.

I can feel the nip in the air in the capital as I get down from the state transport bus and hop into a rickshaw to Anang's house. I try reading the address aloud to the driver, I wrote it so quickly that it's difficult to understand my own writing. After spending three days in the hills, the urge to meet Anang has brought me here. I had the presence of mind to quickly note down his address along with the phone number.

The rickshaw makes several U-turns and I sense that

something is wrong. There is an argument between the rickshaw driver and me. He can sense that I am new to this place and do not know the route. Evening is setting in and I am feeling anxious asking myself, 'How safe is safe? How nice is nice?' Desperate to end this ordeal, I sweet-talk the auto guy into dropping me safely for twice the amount we'd agreed on. If I had fought more, he would have left me stranded on the road.

He's already repeatedly told me that there is no lane like this. Do I have the wrong address? I call him once again hoping this time he will definitely answer the phone. I cross my fingers. 'The person you are trying to reach is currently unavailable. Please try calling again later. Beep. Beep. Beep.' The ringtone goes blank.

I can hear the sound of the rickshaw going further away from me. I stand there looking at a gate guarding a typical Delhi brick building. It has three floors, skirted by balconies, with a few houses dimly lit while others with white tube lights and blaring television sounds in the background. What should I do when I come face to face with him? Should I hug him? Or wait for him to make the first move? Should I ask him why he has not answered his phone, or should I just let it be, now that he is in front of me and has no excuses? What will it be like? I should have picked up something for him. A little gift.

Instead of going to A wing, I take a little breather. I am afraid he will not open the door. I am even more afraid that he will. I decide to take a chance. An awkward, eerie feeling sets in as I climb the stairs of an old building. I want to hug him, kiss him, snuggle and not wake up until noon. I want it all for the rest of my life. That night when we had the conversation under the stars, we both connected, and our personal burdens felt a little lighter. The emptiness of losing a parent, in his case, his father and mother. For me, my mother's death and a father who does exist but only in the most literal sense. And both of us lost a grandfather, perhaps not related by blood in his case but a grandparent all the same.

I am standing in front of an off-white door with the number six written on it. There are three other flats on the same floor. I am confused about which bell to ring since the doors are so close to each other, separated by a single light bulb emitting a foreboding weak light. My hands are trembling as I ask the guard if he knows anyone named Anang. He smells of cheap alcohol and before he can answer, I run away.

The bell makes a strange sound of an ambulance van making its way through heavy traffic. I ring once again but no one seems to be there on the other side. I am heartbroken. So heartbroken that I sit on the steps and cry and cry. He is not here. There is no one called Anang. He was just a dream that happened to me one day and is now gone.

Tears still rolling down my face, I walk down one floor. I walk each step down, thinking, 'Why am I here?' The answer is standing in front of me opening the door of number three, just opposite the last step of the first floor. I bump into a human. The scent is familiar, the aura different. It is him. I look at his eyes which are tired and droopy as if he has been awake for a long time. His wavy hair has grown bushy. Not the man I envisaged last night. This one looks like he has just returned from the Himalayas after a long penance. He shivers as he opens the door. Winter is about to set in. Two scared people are standing in front of each other and one of them has to speak.

'Are you ok, Anang?' I touch his bare arms.

'Ooorja.'

'Can I come inside? You look unwell.'

'Let me in please,' I urge.

I push him aside and step in. Strangely, he does not stop me, although at this point, I am mentally prepared to be stopped and I am also ready to fight back. Why am I doing this? I am in love with a complicated man. The half-drunk watchman brings my bags and places it at the door and looks at us as if it's just another regular couple fight he has seen many times. I pull Anang inside the house, who is still silent, with a plain expression that I am used to by now. At this moment, I don't know how I muster so much strength. I want to make this work.

Anang has not spoken a word and nor have I; we are just two people in a room, with an unknown barrier between them.

Oorja and Anang.
Together. Separate.
Familiar. Unfamiliar.
Yin. Yang.
One coin. Different sides.

He wobbles with pain and looks fragile and I am unable to recognize the person in front of me. It has been a week since I met him. His face looks angry and so is mine. So angry that I want to scream out loud and shake him to bring him to his senses. But he is looking like a lost baby, not knowing where to go. Was this the man I have been visualizing in moments of longing? He is perspiring profusely and plonks himself on the sofa without removing his shoes. I decide to stay the night. I take my bags inside and make his messy bedroom mine. His room is a reflection of his mind—the bedsheet is crumpled; unwashed socks are under the bed with a pile of papers with a dusty office suitcase. This person seems completely different from the man I had met at the estate.

I pick up the stuff lying on the floor to make space to sleep. There are many documents. There are scribbles on a piece of paper which looks like a to-do list. Some notes, stuck on the wall, have fallen off. I pick one of them up, which reads, 'Anang Rajan' with an address on it. This is Rajan uncle's address! The uncle who owns the stationery shop. What is this address doing here?

My hands are trembling. My eyes are going moist and I don't know what is happening right now. I feel numb and my head is a chaotic web of thoughts. Everything spins around me. I open his only steel cupboard. There are more books. Books on forests, insects, birds and a couple of T-shirts and jeans. Some resembling the clothes he was wearing in the estate.

The room is suffocating me. I cross a pile of unwashed glasses and whiskey bottles. Near the window, there are more stacks of papers. All kinds of papers. Newspapers with news of love and hate that hark to the passing of time. Written notes covered in dust. Registers that resemble the ones in my grandfather's house, the kind that was in his hand the day I met him. My vision is slowly blurring. The white papers seem to be reflecting a kaleidoscope of light dancing frenziedly in front of my eyes before slowly turning black. I fall on the floor with sweaty palms, trembling feet and a parched mouth. I am trying to stumble out of my foggy state of mind.

16

Time seems to have paused. I open my eyes in the morning with an intense desire to find some answers. Seeing those old suitcases below the bed, I want to open them and discover what is inside. My still foggy mind tells me something is amiss, but I don't remember anything clearly. The harsh light is hitting my eyes and it's difficult to open them. I get up slowly from the side. The room looks dead, except the self-help quotes of hope pasted on a wall.

> *Be who you are, everybody else is taken.*
> *When you love someone, set them free.*
> *Where there is a will, there is a way.*
> *Trust yourself.*
> *Love yourself more than anyone else.*

The door of the bedroom is closed. Not a movement can be heard. I have a bad cramp in my left leg. I hop across the bed and open the door of the bathroom. The hinges make eerie sounds as I push it. It is dark inside. I switch on a light to see a face suddenly and I scream. Anang looks like a caveman. He does not say anything and instead bangs the bathroom door shut, locking it from inside. I feel a stinging pain on the ankle of my left leg. I bang on the bathroom door hard. I am so angry that I won't hesitate to break the door. I am waiting outside and this moment seems unreal. Two humans who know each other are in a war and god knows why. Am I hallucinating? Why is he behaving so strangely?

I sit on the bed staring at the square lines marking each tile on the floor and tapping my feet impatiently. He finally steps out of the bathroom. Even with the open curtains and the sun showering some hope, he averts his eyes from mine. I follow him to the kitchen. He stops to look back. I stop too, still behind him. I am waiting to see what he is going to do next. He pours some water into the kettle which soon starts boiling, perfectly complementing the anger brewing on his face. I take a step forward and look at him, 'Anang, what's wrong? Why are you not speaking to me? I came here last night. You failed to recognize me. Were you drunk?' I laugh bitterly. He does not find it funny. 'What are you doing here, Oorja?' he finally says, breaking the long silence. I smile and reply, 'I came to meet you.' He opens the drawer to take out a mug. I am trying to form my next words. As I look up, about to ask him what has happened to him, I see a menacing expression on his face. The kettle makes steaming sounds telling us it's done. I step back but I am scared. 'Why did you come here, Oorja?'

'What the hell is wrong with you?' I am furious. 'I came here because I missed you. I wanted to meet you, and hold you and...,' I say as I come closer to him. He is breathing heavily as he looks at me with a piercing gaze. I feel like I am in a mirror glass maze à la Sherlock Holmes. There is a door to get out, but I am not able to find it. Even if I do and open it, I find the next one I must open. He is close to me, looking into my eyes. There is no room to run away. I smile at him when in reality, I am a little afraid of him. Is this the same man I kissed last week? The same man who walked with me under a starlit sky talking about life and death? The same man who protected me from a terrifying dream? Hugged me and gave me warmth? Took care of my grandfather? Who is this man in front of me?

'Anang, I will go, if you tell me what's going on.' Something is not right with him. I can gauge from his eyes, which are pleading that he needs to be taken care of. Anang looks warm, his body warmer. He calms down a little and goes back to his bedroom with the door closed; he has been talking to someone for a while. I can barely hear snatches of the conversation. When he opens the door, I quickly get back to the kitchen. He comes and sits beside me silently. He keeps looking at the phone as if he is waiting for a call. I ask no questions.

My eyes shift to the kettle which has stopped making noise. I move forward and make him the black coffee that he was making for himself. He takes the coffee mug from me with shivering hands. Sitting there in the corner of the kitchen on a wooden stool, Anang is not my Mr Big Hands anymore. He is a timid-looking man, like a fish in an ocean waiting to be saved from the monsters of the sea.

I cannot see him in pain as he puts his warm head on my shoulder.

I am waiting in the dark for some light.

He asks me, 'Will there be a better tomorrow? How long am I supposed to wait?'

'After every night, there is a morning of hope,' I say with love in my eyes.

Anang stares at me trying to speak to me but his eyes are drowsy, he stands to walk but his weak feet won't listen. I pull him on one shoulder to his bedroom with difficulty and put him on the bed. I tend to him with a cold ice cloth and apply balm to his aching muscles. He snuggles after a while, not leaving my hands. In the loneliness of a dead room, Anang needs the warmth of a touch that says, 'I care', as I put a blanket on him and give him a kiss of love on his forehead.

Anang seems visibly uneasy as he sleeps in the bedroom; I clean the house as if it is mine. I have longed to stay with him and now I am unwelcome in his house. What am I even doing here? I can easily walk out and consider Anang another forgotten chapter in my life. Why am I still here? I keep asking myself. None of this makes any sense. I am intrigued by the letter with my home address in Lucknow. Who is Anang Rajan? This mystery has to reveal itself.

The doorbell rings. Anang is in a deep sleep. The doorbell rings again and I am a little unsure whether to open the door. The person on the other side then starts banging the door. It must be something important. I go to the door and look through the peep hole. An elderly gentleman is standing there looking frantic. After ringing the bell once more, I see him calling someone on his phone. It is Anang's phone that rings inside. I go towards the ringing on the phone and find it in his pocket. I try to take the phone slowly without disturbing him. 'Dr. Sandeep Bansal' flashes on the screen.

I go back to the front door and finally open it. 'Why did you take so long to open the door?' I do not answer. He walks right in and attempts to gently wake Anang up. But Anang is fast asleep and does not wake up. The doctor holds his hand and checks his pulse, touches his head and then stomach, then heaves a long sigh. He turns to wake him up again. I am fretting now, wondering what has happened to Anang. The doctor slaps him on the face. He then asks me to get water. I quickly go into the kitchen and get a bottle of water. Handing over the bottle, I ask, 'What happened, Doc?' The doctor is trying to wake him up and seems frantic now. 'We have to take him to the hospital right away and put him under observation.' He checks Anang's pulse rate again.

The ambulance noise takes over the sound of my heart beating out of my chest.

17

I have a lot of questions for Dr Sandeep Bansal. We are sitting in the ambulance opposite each other while Anang lies in between, his chest moving up and down slowly as he breathes feebly.

In the closed bedroom, Anang had apparently called Dr Bansal to visit him urgently. He arrived half an hour after Anang had gone to sleep. As we both look at Anang breathing laboriously, Dr Bansal says with a lot of concern, 'My clinic is in the next lane and Anang used to visit me every time his blood pressure was not in the desired range. In the recent past, it had been fluctuating and we would curb it by increasing the dosage of medicines. He seems to be getting better, but only time will tell if it will be possible to control it or not. This time around while Anang was travelling back from the hills, he caught a fever which he chose to ignore, thinking it's a regular flu with the changing season and will subside soon. But last evening, his fever increased which got uncontrollable and led to seizures. I sensed a threat that this is beyond the usual. We got the blood test done immediately, followed by a cerebrospinal fluid analysis and found out that Anang had contracted cerebral malaria. I had no time to waste and called Anang a couple of times at night, but he did not pick his phone. This afternoon, he called me saying he had severe fever with unbearable headache and was disoriented from last evening in spite of the medication. But I wonder how all this was happening before you and it went unnoticed.' He looks at me with disbelief as if we have a long association and accuses me of not noticing that Anang had contracted high fever. He looked unwell but how could I guess it was an extreme case? All this was too much information and difficult for me to digest. 'I am Oorja, Anang's friend,' I introduce myself.

The man I met a couple of days ago looks so weak now. Dr Bansal tells me that he is worried that there is a possibility that Anang might go into coma. Before I can even ask him anymore, we reach our destination. A board at the hospital reads, 'A doctor can heal if God wants to.' What if Anang never comes out of this dreadful illness?

The sight of hospitals scares me. The smell of medicines and syringes takes me back to my last days in New York. I had ended up in a hospital then and I am inside one again. Anang is put on a stretcher and in the blink of an eye, is taken inside. I am stopped at the emergency door, there are some forms I need to fill for Anang. Who am I to him? Can I take responsibility that if something happens to him, I won't blame the doctors? What is the date today? What is the time now? Today is my father's birthday. I cannot control my tears as the drops fall on the paper. A nurse comes to me with Anang's phone and wallet which was in his jeans. She pacifies me and tells me that everything would be okay. 'Your husband is here. Few months back, husband's mother was here,' I look at her in confusion. HUSBAND? 'This time mother is not here. But wife is here.' She smiles and pats my head. 'Pray, my child.' Her way of comforting me, for whatever reason, is full of love, so I do not correct her.

I sit in the waiting area, anxiously thinking about the doctors and nurses who are caring for Anang. All around me are people who have a loved one here and they are all waiting. In an abnormal environment like this, even the strongest become weak, waiting for positive answers. What if Anang goes into an uncommunicative state? What would I do then? I often wonder what Amma must have thought in those final moments of her life. Was she afraid of dying? There were so many things she wanted to do but most of them took a backseat due to the responsibilities of family. Did anyone ever ask her how she wanted to live her life? Has anyone asked anyone here, sitting and waiting for a dear one's life, what they actually want? His phone and wallet are in my hands and I try to convince myself, 'I am ready for whatever is in store for me.'

Anang's phone is staring at me; it reminds me that the phone number I had given to the cops in the hills may not exist and they have no other alternative number to connect with me if they find some news about my father. Who could have thought in human history that a phone can bring so much sorrow and joy? Giving good news and bad news. Breakups and makeups. It can all happen in one phone call. I see many people speaking on the phone, some frantic calls and others, calming. I have carried the crumpled paper with me to check where I had written down the cop's number. In one corner, right below some other words, I find it. My father's unclear words now flash in front of me. I can comprehend each word that together forms a clear headline.

Sudha Submission Deadline
May 31st

What submission?

I have to first finish the task at hand. Call the cop. His number is saved as COP Nainital and I never asked his name. How foolish of me! I dial the number using Anang's simple phone which is not password protected.

'Hello? Sir, I am Oorja Chaturvedi, daughter of Vishal Chaturvedi. The one who is missing.' I can hear some strange voices in the background. He is listening to me but at the same time, talking to another person, I assume another cop. 'Madam, we have called you so many times. Your case will be closed if you don't come here right away. We have found some evidence that may be connected to your father's case. But to be sure, you need to come here to see if he is your father,' he continues without letting me speak, 'We have called you so many times! If your phone is switched off, why did you give us that number? I wanted to give you the information that might be connected to your father.' I interrupt him now, 'I did not know this phone would be unreachable.' I keep quiet for a while. 'Hello Madam. Hellooo?' My voice is sounding tense now, 'What is it?' There is a call on his other line. Speaking to both of us, he is impatient now, 'You come here, madam, we talk then. Also, please get some cash. There is a pending payment for closing file.' Before I can say anything, I hear a blank tone on the other side. I am irritated now and feel like throwing something.

'Dear Doctor Bansal, I need to rush to Nainital for some urgent work. I don't know when I will be back. I will connect through Anang's phone. I will also take care of the hospital expenses when I am back. If you could connect with any of his relatives, if there are any, that would be great. I am no one to him, in case you thought otherwise.' I end the letter with my name. The nurse who called me Anang's wife is standing by the reception, yapping on the phone. I walk towards her and hand the letter to her, categorically asking her to give it to the Doctor. She cattily tells me, 'You send message. Doctor will read it.' I am angry now and half-shout at her, 'No, I don't want to send message. And patient is not my husband.' She wants some gossip. I give it to her. I walk away, leaving her dumbstruck.

///

I am waiting for my turn at the police station looking at the far-off mountains, I think about how sometimes, it rains and sometimes, the sun shines through the clouds but the mountains stand still. Unlike the sturdy mountains, the unexpectedness of the past few days in my life has shaken me. I feel like I am a pawn in a game of chess; I have no idea what move life is going to play next. I think about the turns my life has taken and wonder if routine would have been better. Doing the same job for years and years, like my father. My mother cooking, cleaning, eating, attending to my father, like clockwork. Just like the cop sitting in front of me talking on the phone while I stare at him, noticing his overgrown moustache, the threads of his faded uniform. His name is tagged for life on his chest pocket, 'Ramsingh Karawat.' 'Inspector Saab, how much more time?' I ask, just to catch his attention, which is consumed by a couple having a cat fight in front of us. The wife is screaming to the high heavens, but the man does not budge.

As a child, I used to fall on the ground while running on purpose so I could get my mother's attention and have her fuss over me. My father did not care. 'It will become okay, it's just a scratch, apply some cream and it will be okay by tomorrow. You need to learn to be strong and not cry about such small things' He was unable to understand that I was doing this to gain love from him. But it did not work. I grew up to ask for attention in a different way. I wanted everyone to like me, so I became a 'Yes' person. Yes, for everything. The 'yes' has hurt me enough that I slowly learned to say no too. A cup of chai suddenly falls on the floor drawing the attention of everyone in the room. I feel for the wife who is suddenly alone despite her husband being around.

They walk towards the door, their story unsolved and to be continued. After watching them go, I stand in front of the inspector and patiently request him for a chat. He pleads for another ten minutes. His morning breakfast and chai is yet to be finished. 'Why don't you just tell me so I can leave? What is this suspense?' I say; I am fuming now. I barge out of the room angrily. They must have not seen a woman like this before. The fatigue sets in. Between leaving America, my mother's memories, my father missing and taking the responsibility of a sick person I met a couple of days back, I am bone tired. I scream loudly, so loudly that all the men in uniform come running outside. The driver of an ambulance parked nearby also starts to move towards me.

Ramsingh Karawat is standing behind me, along with two other lady cops, just in case I need to be held and sent to the hospital. But no such thing happens. I am calm now. He asks me whether I would like another cup of tea and I nod saying yes. His affable smile gives me some relief as we walk on the lane that goes uphill to the police department junkyard. In front of me lie derailed, crashed, unused cars parked in piles. Inspector Ramsingh stops there to look at an off-white one which has the number plate belonging to Lucknow. My eyes move along with him. 'So, why am I here?' He stares at the sky, like a slow movie taking its own sweet time to come to the point. I am in no hurry now as I gauge he has something to tell me and I suspect the news isn't good. I ask Ramsingh politely, 'So did my father meet with an accident and the locals found his car upside down? The locals took him to the hospital, right?' He looks down and finally speaks to me, looking into my eyes, 'We took him to a morgue.'

I am strangely calm and do not feel anything at this moment at all. I walk towards the car and see it from inside. The driver's seat is crushed.

'I won't believe until I see and identify,' I tell Ramsingh in disagreement. I walk away, leaving the inspector with a doubt that what he claims may not be true. In all these chaotic thoughts, I just have one lingering guilt, 'I wish I had spent enough time with my father.' The inspector follows me and shouts from behind, 'Madam, please sit in the police jeep. We need to take you to the morgue for identification.' The afternoon sun is hitting my eyes and I wear my dark glasses. Behind those glasses, my emotions are churning. The same emotions that I refused to show to some strange inspector who has given me this devastating news.

One more hospital ride, but this time it is in a police car. It stinks of fights that did not resolve. Of unending greed. Of unsatisfied lives. Of incomplete dreams. Of a sudden story which appears in your life that pulls the rug from under your feet with a sudden, merciless yank. My father's forgotten face stares at me with his emotionless sentences. 'You need to be strong, Oorja. This is no reason to cry.'

A man sitting on a chair outside the morgue in the hospital asks me, 'Are you his daughter?' I nod and he hands me a paper to sign. The man gives me a register to sign, asking me to close the file here itself if my father is dead. I sign but still refuse to believe what I am about to see.

All I think about are the could-haves and should-haves. I could have told him about my woes. How much I wanted him to hug me sometimes and talk to me lovingly like a father. How much I wanted him to know more about me. I could have spoken freely, and he could have asked why I was always so angry.

It was because of you, my dear father. If you had loved me enough, I would not care how much love the world gave me. I would not care about being alone if I had you on my side. You hurt me as much as I hurt you, dear father. You left halfway in my story and I will need to take it through to the end.

The evening somehow feels darker, gloomier as the clouds descend. My father's clothes, wallet and a briefcase are handed over to me. The inspector seems genuinely sorry for me, even though he is used to seeing death in his job. The last piece to the puzzle of my missing father has been found. I walk along the long corridor in peace. I am an orphan and it is as if I am on the outside looking at myself. I am suddenly not responsible for anyone but myself. I am not answerable to anyone but myself. I went through Anang's phone the previous night and found messages to the doctor, photographs of the forest. A picture of his mother, not father. But nothing that would help me connect the dots. Perhaps it is time to go back to America now and start a new journey. A panting man from the morgue interrupts my thoughts. 'This was found in the car tucked in between the gear. We cannot keep your father's ring even if we want to. It's against the Almighty's wish.' I look at the moonstone ring made in silver. He walks away and I scream at him, 'This is a mistake! It's not my father's ring.' He is gone. I keep looking at the stone, shining like a bright moon with dust on it.

With the policeman by my side, I light the fire to my father's body. I see his ashes going up to the sky. What must he be thinking when he drove rashly and crashed himself in the valley? The first time, he had killed my mother. The second time, he killed himself. My eyes burn with the smoke and the ashes, the sky is grey with clouds and the sounds of lightning merge with the crackling sounds of the fire burning. I stand here too, burning in turn, looking for answers.

> *When the sun and moon meet*
> *In between the mountains*
> *In between the sea.*
> *In the spark of love,*
> *you will see a stream.*
> *A hope.*
> *It never ends.*

The last words of my father on the note written for me answers one of my questions but there are many more lingering ones. I throw my father's note into the fire and let it burn.

18

I have been waiting a long time for Anang to wake up, but he does not move an inch. His face, still without a smile, is unnerving. His rising fever has reached his brain, causing unconsciousness. If he is in blank state, I feel nothing too. I am numb.

I do want to know what is wrong with him. Gauging that he was going through a hard phase, I am wondering what was bothering a man who was perfectly fine a week ago. Strangely enough, I am not thinking much about my father but about this unconscious man in front of me. He has a calm expression and looks like the one I can fall in love with over and over again. But something is missing. Why is he hiding who he is? Come to think of it, he never hid it actually. It was I who never bothered to ask him his second name. I never asked him where his hometown is. Is it at all surprising that I hardly know any personal details about the man? Often, we make up things on our own, without confirming the truth. We assume that this is the way it is. Did I ask what my mom was feeling? Did I know any more about my father? I assumed he is someone I cannot connect with, and I let it be the reason I spent my whole life without him. I saw his peaceful face and in that one moment, I asked myself, 'What if I had asked?' What if I had asked how he was feeling after my mother was gone? What if I had asked why he behaved the way he did? May be there are many reasons why we often forget to ask the real questions and get lost in assumptions. Now my mother and father are both gone forever, and I will never be able to ask them the questions I want to.

His eyes are closed as I sit beside him. I know him. But I don't know him at all. Why am I sitting here? I start crying uncontrollably. I want my father back. I want my mother back. I want everyone I love in my life back. All alone now, a torrent of tears gush out and I feel helpless. The nurse next to the doctor tries to hold me but the doctor asks her to leave and lets me cry. Sometimes we don't cry enough to let out our pain. Crying can be cathartic. We need to cry till we feel okay.

'You don't know who he is?' Dr Bansal, who has just returned from his clinic, asks me doubtfully.

'No, I don't know!' I am looking down, still crying.

'Are you delusional?' He is stern and can see that I have no control over my emotions.

'My parents are dead. I don't know what my future is going to be like. I don't know when I will go back and restart.' I stand up and look at the doctor angrily, 'I don't know who this man is. I know nothing about him. I only met him at my grandfather's home when I went to spend some time with him. He too is gone. Do you understand, Doctor?'

I am so angry that I could break things in there. I leave the room and rush down the steps with my father's suitcase. I slip and twist my leg. The suitcase opens and a bundle of papers goes flying all across the corridor. I gather myself up and frantically start collecting those papers which have a lot written on it. I am crying profusely yet again, and the tears pour over the words written in my mother's handwriting.

The Changing Nature in The Internet Age
By Sudha Chaturvedi
PhD (Botany)
Final Year Thesis

My hands reach out to a big envelope with the address of Professor Chandran Vishwa (Botany), Delhi University on it. I tear apart the envelope to read the typed script of my mother's handwritten thesis. People walk by. I sit in the corner of the steps with my mother's life's work in my hands. Another letter mentions the submission deadline—15th December. Please forgive me, dear father and mother. Only if I could tell you this before.

The moon talks
To unbind and revive.
Where the old is woven beneath the threads of a fair chance.
To rise, fall and rise again.
This is the law of the changing cycle.
A beginning of a new thought.
Unfolding an old self in a new you.

I stand up, there is a sprain in my ankle, and it hurts but I don't pay it any attention. The time is 11:30 and it is the 18th of December. I am three days late but not too late. The doctor is calling me. I pick the call this time. 'Doctor, I have something important to finish. Can I meet you in the evening back here?' I cut the phone, not waiting for him to give me an answer.

The University is not too far. For the first time, I am doing something important and meaningful. I take an auto outside the hospital and reach in under 20 minutes. I walk inside the gate with a suitcase of a dream that my mother had visualized forever, and my father helped her fulfill. There will always be doubts about people and the way they behave. Do they really mean what they say? We expect people to behave in a certain way but is that the right thing to do? I ask for Professor Chandran Vishwa and I am guided to a room with his name on it. He looks at me doubtfully. 'I am sorry for the late submission of my mother's final year thesis.' It feels like he has been waiting for me for ages. 'I am sorry to hear about your mother. Your father could not come? He called me a few days back saying he was on his way to submit the thesis which your mother had left. But there was no call after that.' I stand quietly for a few seconds and then say, 'My father is no more.' The professor is speechless. He is in front of a woman who had just lost her father and mother. One lost her life coming back after her year-end submissions, the other left this world when he was about to submit his wife's final dream.

'You are a good daughter,' he empathizes with me, taking my mother's thesis.

'I am just doing what my mother would have wanted me to,' I reply.

For the first time, I feel like I have done something right.

19

I have not known myself for very long now. Sometimes I am who I am. Sometimes, I am who others see me as. I am two people in one. There are days I feel perfectly normal, but that lasts only like a honeymoon period and then everything is gone; I have spurts of good and bad days, altering from one phase to the other. The trigger of a memory makes me someone else. I myself don't know who I am today. I want to be in control. I am Anang Rajan, the naturalist who wanted to do a lot more with his life than to be put on a saline drip, which gives me hope that I will wake up to see myself as a normal person and not destroy myself unknowingly with a fiery rage.

The one voice in my mind keeps telling me that I must do this because Vishal killed my mother. Crashing his car into another because he was speeding is killing, I believe. I don't know. But this voice in my head keeps telling me I cannot keep quiet for long. I tell him that it happened, and I should move on. But he keeps coming back. I cannot get over Vishal, Oorja's father. The night is worn out today. My stomach is squirming, and Oorja is in my house. She smiles and gives me black coffee which I was making for myself to subside the growing fever. Oorja is talking constantly, altering words, saying that I met her a few days back. I look at her, want to speak to her but her eyes remind me of her father, Vishal. I am feverish and fuming as she speaks to me but the calmer side of me knows her and I am trying to regulate my rage.

I don't want to be here. In the noise of the ambulance and flashing red light, I am trapped in my own paranoia, caught in the web of wrath that makes it impossible to see the good among the bad. A new night of hope in the circle of life. I want to cry but I want to laugh too. I will open my eyes to see her and hear her voice uttering sweet nothings.

I can feel Dr Bansal holding me and trying to pacify me. I can hear Oorja asking the doctor whether I will survive. How I wish I could cry out loud and tell her how much I love her and want to spend the rest of my life with her! She will take me in her arms and get me out of here. We will stay happy together and I promise I will work on myself. It's a strange situation to be in. To fall in love with the daughter of the man I hate. I wish I could tell her now, but my body is aching with a rush of blood into my brains.

My heartbeat slows. The noises around me diminish.

It is nothing but destiny that we found the true meaning of love. Oorja keeps looking at my angry face which will soon subside to a calmer one. She will kiss me goodbye with tears in her eyes that shine like dew drops. 'See you on the other side, Darling. I will sleep now.' I hold Oorja's hands with a smile of comfort.

20

Anang has this strange maturity I have not seen in the many men I have dated. His silence speaks a lot. The evening was about my sense of responsibility towards my mother. I came back straight here to see him again. I am getting used to the eerie silence that we have developed between us. I am in love.

The love I saw in his eyes has not disappeared, although his face is different from the night I brought him to the hospital. That man is gone like a leaf that falls off from a tree to never come back. He asks me in his half-conscious state, eyes closed, 'How are you feeling?' 'Fragile,' I reply. The monitor shows lines that are going down. I do not bother to call the doctor. I just want to see him breathe through the tubes of life. I fix my eyes and put my head on his chest, moving gently with each inhalation and exhalation.

The moonstone ring lies in a little pocket inside my bag. The sound of the machines and the white tube light make it a perfect setting to stare at this ring. I hold his big hands in mine. They are emitting warmth; each finger is well designed by god. They say that when you have long fingers, you will be a good artist. Was he a good artist? As I am caressing his fingers, I notice a ring mark on his ring finger. A discolored round mark with a square rim design in the middle. Not a tattoo which symbolizes a significant memory of your life. Not a mole which brings in luck as per where it is placed. This one is lighter than his actual skin tone, a stone ring that was worn for a long time. It resembles the moonstone ring which was my father's and later given to me. But how can it be mine when it was never my father's?

My father never believed in the science of astrology. He was a firm believer of karma. You reap what you sow. My mother used to go to the place of worship to find solace, but he never indulged her faith. My mother and I used to pray to a little photo of God stuck inside my mother's cupboard which my father never opened. His lifelong interest in archeology and the physical evidence of history and the earth was the reason behind his aversion to religion and prayer. He did not have too many friends; he could not even get along with my grandfather. He never got along with me. He was one who loved himself the most and was selfish enough to always think of his happiness first.

Who is this man and why does this ring fit him so well? This moonstone ring that was found in my deceased father's car.

⁂

It is a full moon night. A beautiful night. My mind goes back to the place where I belong, the place from where I started, my grandfather's house. The house must be dimly lit, with a memory of a time that went by teaching me that there are no ifs and buts in the way you move in life. A touch of moon caressing the night sky almost urges me to not read anything between the lines and wait to discover him peeling his emotions like an onion. The day he said, 'see you' in my ears was his way of saying goodbye. And when we met again, he came like a cyclone without any warning and together, we drowned in the unexplainable aftermath.

'He is suffering from fits of anger that he is unable to control,' Dr Bansal explains to me why this man behaves the way he does. I agitatedly retort, 'I don't even know who he is. How would I know what he is suffering from?'

'Why are you lying, Oorja? Are you saying you don't even know that he is your mother's best friend's son?'

Yes, it is true. I am lying. Because now, I know who Anang really is. I have been thinking about this over and over in my head and I finally piece together all the stories I have heard. Amma had neighbours who were as close as family, but I had never met them because I never went back home. I had heard about her best friend Sarita a couple of times from Amma but listened to those conversations only half-heartedly. I knew about Sarita aunty's son but never bothered to ask his name and she never mentioned either. In conversations with my parents, I would selectively hear what my mother had to say and remain silent with my father.

Sarita aunty's son Anang was very keen to become an environmentalist and get into Indian Forest Services and every time my mother would go to meet my grandfather, he used to accompany her and spend time with my grandfather. He would also take care of the house which had partly become a guest house due to my mother's absence, since she needed to be around my father.

Sometimes, you know who you are and sometimes, you don't. Anang and I are a lot similar in that case. The man who had an ambition got lost when he had to encounter someone he wanted to avoid. That night when my father was driving my mother back to Lucknow from Delhi after finishing her university documentation, it was not just the two of them. She was with her best friend, Sarita. Every time Amma used to travel to Delhi, Sarita aunty joined her to visit her son who was studying to get a seat in the forest service. But there was something more. She was also visiting Dr Bansal who was recommended by my grandfather as the Doctor's father was in the Indian Forest Services. Anang had been increasingly getting anger fits, which started while he was preparing for his entrance exams. The bouts were increasing with time but Anang insisted that he would stay in Delhi in the care of Dr Bansal. His mother could not stay with him but in the daily calls, he would assure everything was fine. Whenever his mood struck him, he used to visit Baba to find calm in the stillness of the jungle. He tried to become better and was improving until that morning, while writing his entrance papers, he had a fit in the exam hall, leaving unanswered questions and a bleak future in the forest services in its trail.

Around his mother who had come to visit him and stayed for two days, he was as calm as the sea on a good day, when he saw the smile on her face. She was truly anxious and felt that she could not leave her only son all by himself. She made his favourite food and finally, convinced him to come back home and forget about these entrance exams. She was sending him to Australia. Having lost his father Rajan two years back to a heart attack, they had sold his stationery shop to save enough for his education. His father's pension as a professor and also her teacher's job in higher secondary school was good enough for her to get him settled.

That night in his house while he was asleep, I had read the strewn notes. All of them read, 'Anang Rajan' with a

Lucknow address on it. It was Rajan uncle's address. The uncle who was a professor and who owned Rajan stationery shop. The same stationery shop where I was given the keys to my house. I later learned that the person I met, who I thought was Mr Rajan, was actually the new owner.

Anang was convinced but the thought of leaving his mother and going so far troubled him for she was the only one who understood him. But she was adamant and promised to join him after he was settled. The cryptic questions and the half answers I listened to, made me assume certain untold conversations. Anang is not Gagan Bhaiya's son.

I suddenly come back to my present where Dr Bansal is sitting next to Anang and pacifying him like his own son. 'A dent in a glass looks beautiful, failing the entrance exams for forest services is not the end. It was a beginning of a new destiny waiting for you.'

I again think of that phone call on that dark conspiring night that Dr Bansal described to me. It was his mother's phone with my father howling. He asked, 'Why are you calling from my mother's phone? What happened to your phone?'

'It's dead,' my father replied.

'What happened to my mother?'

'She is dead.'

The phone went blank.

Anang Rajan went blank.

21

The accident left a scar for life. My father was not arrested since it was an accident that could not be controlled. Whom do you blame—the truck which came in front of you or your destiny? I was the chosen line joining the dots.

Anang's phone is as mysterious as him. A number his mother, my mother, the Doctor, my grandfather and my father had. The same unknown number which flashed as missed calls on my father's phone. The same messages which read, 'I am here waiting for you,' with no name. When I dialled this number, it said unavailable. The same number I was called from by the lawyers. The same number I kept dialing when I was in Delhi. They all led to an unknown person I now know—Anang.

The ring matched. The ring which was found in my father's car. The case was closed because the police felt it was a routine accident.

My father had reached Delhi on the morning I was travelling to my grandfather's estate. He wanted to meet Anang and give him my mother's thesis for submission but before that, they were going to the mountain house to finish some important work. He wanted to make that closed house a guest house and felt Anang would be a good help. They met as if everything was forgotten. Memories have a way of coming back in some form.

That accident was a night which he never wanted to remember. The bouts of anger, the panic attacks, the day he spent in hospital slowly became a part of him. He seemed to be two people in one. When one was erased, the other emerged. He tried to calm himself but like a shadow, it kept following. On some days, he did well, dreaming about his studies in Australia. On other days, he was doubtful of every person who met him. For some reason, he could always remember Dr Bansal. Even in his two facets, he could remember him. Sometimes, he remembered his childhood and the food he liked. Sometimes, he was normal but quiet.

Now when I look back at those couple of days we spent together, I remember some strangeness in him. Emotionally, he was unpredictable and gave me the hot and cold treatment. Later, I learnt the whole story.

Anang met my father with growing resentment. As soon as they hit the mountains, a strange feeling was evoked in Anang. The fire of the other side of him was turning him into what he did not want to be. He insisted that he drive the car. My father refused. He insisted again. And when my father did not allow, he pushed my father to the corner of the car which was now taking hairpin turns before it slipped to the valley. Anang pushed himself out of the car and when he saw the carnage, he started running in horror to finally catch a bus from the next stop in the village.

Anang got on to the bus but remembered to reach my grandfather's house. His memory kept fluctuating according to the condition of his mind. It seemed as if he had an out-of-body experience.

Later, I had opened the door to an angry man who roared like a wounded animal. The words of my late father come to my mind.

The leaves meet the sky
In this union they believe.
The nature of life
Not about you and me.
The trust in us
takes me to you
To the shadows of a dense forest.
My destiny.

LEFTOVER

He is breathing hard, the lines on the ECG machine is going up and down. I sit there, consoling myself, 'This too shall pass'. The bloodsucking mosquitoes have eaten away at his brain like termites eating up every piece of wood they find.

I promise myself to celebrate the departed every year for the people who have left me at different times. I think of the various moments I had with them. The forced conversations I had with my mother even when I felt she is talking too much. The days when I did not want to speak to her. The days I missed her. The days when I wanted to scream at my father. The day when I wanted to leave my parents forever. The day I wanted to never come back. The day I met the man I was never meant to be with. The day he hurt me with a mixture of love and hate. The day I was in the hospital bed. The day I stood on the middle of a crowded street and howled. The day I landed in this country reluctantly. The day I entered the house of awareness. The day I went through the circle of life on the Ganges, cleansing my soul. The day I met my grandfather. The day I looked into the eyes of a man, which spoke of untold stories. The day I renounced the world once again.

I will sit by the window and pray for them. I will read their names like chanting a mantra for the divine. After all, it was because of my parents that I am here. It was she who bore the seed of love.

I will remember it all. The years of togetherness. The happiness. The love. The fights. The arguments. The long endless discussions. Nothing meant anything in the war of words. A volcanic eruption that threw all these memories off. Now all that remains is this empty feeling, a feeling deep inside me that things will be okay. There is stillness. Chaos. Eagerness. Temptation. And then we wait for that one moment, for that black emotional cloud to burst into drops of happiness again. This is the full circle of life.

I am just a parasite singing a song of destiny, leaving every single memory to fuse and light my life like a shooting star. I strangely feel nothing, no pain, no sorrow. I laugh aloud, so loud, that I cry. I am in intense pain, without which I am incomplete. I am ecstatic to close this door of pain and begin again.

MAPPING LOVE

The water is cold, and I am floating on a river nestled in the mountains, looking at the deep blue open sky. Holding Anang, happiness ripples in my heart, caressing my soul and singing a song of hope. Life is different today, amid the mountains in the small home which my father built for my mother. Now it belongs to me and Anang. He is a strong tree of hope; every time the colour red pops in his eyes he swiftly recovers like a bird spreading its wings to fly in an open sky. Love is the answer to everything, and I have taken this as my responsibility to add everyday joy for us. He recognizes that we are meant to be; we just need to give a chance for the sunrise to step into our lives. The forest calls out to him every day, in due time he promises to go back. We visit our guest house occasionally to look after it. Sometimes, we take decisions on the spur of the moment but later question ourselves, 'What's our purpose in life?'

I found mine in the middle of the vast field with vegetables growing, living with nature, swimming almost every day. He holds my hands and teaches me how to navigate myself in the caresses of a cold river that takes away all the forbidden words of negativity. The jungle birds seem to tell us to live our best lives today and not run anywhere. Even while making love, he touches my lips, looks at my face as if he has not seen me for a while. His hands brush against my skin and we immerse in our little world of forgotten past. The fruits of love grow with our learnings from the earth, healing our mind and body. The mountains change their mood for us and whenever we step out, we feel only sunshine, even on a rainy morning. A piece of land and the cryptic words on the paper my father had planned for me accidentally changed my destiny.

Who is right?
Who is wrong?
That is for no one to decide.
Who we are to judge?
For he who started the beginning,
Had the right to end the way he wants it too.
That speaks of forgiveness.
A life that is a bright star.
Of happiness.
A way of life.
A new beginning.

ACKNOWLEDGEMENTS

All our lives are spent in finding our purpose in life and living a life of joy. My purpose was to find words about the matters of the heart and mind, my own and of many like me who nurture such dreams. In my path where wildflowers have grown, I need to be grateful for many who have always believed in me.

It starts from here. Thank you, Nitesh for being my strongest backbone and cheerleader in all my never-ending to-do dreams. For always silently watching me as I wrote for hours and when I was stuck with no words in sight. To my girl and boy, Amaarisa and Aaradhya, who are the sources of my inspiration and hope that one day, we will discuss books with passion. My movie buff, music lover mother, Lakshmi who does not read but makes sure I write so that she can find another reason to be proud of me. My father, Dr Veeramani who taught me to embrace philosophy and arts of all kinds and to love Mozart as well as MS Subbulakshmi. To my bibliophile father-in-law, Dr Brahma Dutta Tiwari, who is watching over me from the sky, guiding me with his words of love. My loving brother-in-law, Brahmesh and sister-in-law, Mukta who constantly support my dreams. My aunt Geeta who introduced reading to me with a second-hand four-in-one book in my teens. My uncle and aunt, Ramki and Urmila, the ones who gave me the courage to make my own choices that made me the first one to go to art school in a family of intellectuals.

My dearest yoga teacher Bhavani who is also a mother saviour, guiding my heart chakra, helping me be the best I can. My brother, Sanjay Shetty who adopted me and gave me the chance to throw my sisterly tantrums. He also taught me a few kick-boxing moves to use, if needed. My dearest Ronitaa, the one who can see through me even in my silence. Danish, my friend for life, who always feels I can accomplish more and constantly gives his one-line advice on the random ideas I share with him without thinking whether he has the time to hear me out. Dr Rashmi Shetty, a sister who finds time from her busy schedule and spoils me with her love.

My 'mad' group—Sherry, Radhika, Nikhil, Shweta, Piyush, Trishna, Abhishek, Junita—which makes me laugh with joy and comforts me in my sorrow. KV Sridhar, with his encouragement, I shifted from advertising to making movies and writing a novel now. Varun Shetty, my forever cool-headed problem solver, adding joy as we walk together with similar work ethic, building our dream company Earthsky Pictures. Bimal Parekh, my pillar of strength, teacher and advisor, who also feels I need to keep sowing seeds of my creativity that makes him feel a sense of pride.

Ronnie Screwvala, who has always given hope to a creative mind trying to find her purpose in life. Ekta Kapoor and Ruchikaa Kapoor Sheikh who believe in my ideas and passion for storytelling more than I do. My sunshine friends in the movies who are always ready to hear an idea and answer my questions in my quest to continue my constant learning. My talented marketing, digital and publicity partners who walk along with me as one team, spreading so much positivity.

Simar, my editor and dear friend, who encouraged me to write this book three years back and continues to ask me about my next one. We can discuss books and life for hours with a regular weekly video call that makes my day. My gratitude to Kapish Mehra, who has followed up many times on my writing and has faith in my ideas without asking too many questions. Thank you also to Yamini Chowdhury and Saswati Bora for owning this piece of love and giving it life. Bena Sareen, for giving her valuable suggestions to the cover design. Vasundhara Raj Baigra, for thinking innovative ways of marketing and breaking set patterns. The entire team at Rupa who worked tirelessly till the end to make sure this book is seen on shelves, both online and offline.

Mrs Sudha Murty, my hero who inspires me every day with her humble, honest attitude and service to people. My staff of over a decade who make life easy for me. So many well-wishers who silently encourage me with their kind words. The various travels, be it the sea, forests or the mountains where paragraphs were written, the places that provided comfort to this story.

The pandemic made me write, opening a world of unexpected thoughts that made me realize the value of the fragile human life. This book is for the ones who have fought on the frontlines. Because of you, I could sit in the comfort of my home and write. Valuing nature, and the meaning it gives, always has a way of calming the human mind. To all the souls across the world who strived to rise again, came together and fought against the dreaded pandemic in this tragic period. Because of your humanity and light, an invincible force makes me hope for a beautiful earth that grows love every day.

My ashes with yours into the river of eternity,
Until we meet again, my dear one.
From where your divine love flows into various avatars.
Like the first ray of sun,
Shining on the white, slow mountains.
Reflecting your light, my dear one!
You walked this far.
The leaves meet the sky
In this union, they believe.
The nature of life
Is not about you and me.
But the trust in us
Takes me along with you
To the shadows of a dense forest.
My destiny.
When the sun and moon meet
In between the mountains
In between the sea.
In the spark of love
you will see a stream.
A hope.
That never ends.

Made in the USA
Monee, IL
03 May 2026